Beautiful Cities and Landmarks
Mosaic World Geography Coloring Book for Adults
Color by Number

By Color Questopia Coloring Books

Thank you
for your purchase!

**Claim your FREE digital copy of our
Highlight Reel Color By Number Book:**

Check out our website: colorquestopia.com

**Join our Facebook group:
facebook.com/colorquestopia**

Follow us on Instagram: @colorquestopia

**Did you enjoy this book?
Please leave us a review!**

https://geni.us/cqreview

Color By Number Tips

1. **Relax and have fun**

   Let your cares slip away as you color the images. Take your time. Coloring is a meditative activity and there's no wrong way to do it. Feel free to color as you listen to music, watch TV, lounge in bed- do whatever relaxes you most! You can also color while you're out and about- on the train or at a cafe- take the book with you anywhere you go. Coloring is therapeutic and is great for stress relief and relaxation!

2. **Colors corresponding to each number are shown on the back cover of the book**

   Each number corresponds to a color shown on the back of the book. You can match the color as closely as you like- but feel free to change the color or the shade if you don't have the exact color match- that's totally fine. Although this is a color by number book, it's completely okay to get creative and color the images with whichever colors you like and have. The numbers are there to be a guide and to allow you to color without having to focus your energy on choosing colors.

3. **Choose your coloring tools**

   Everyone has their favorite coloring markers, crayons, pencils, pens- even paints! Feel free to color with any tool that you like! If you choose markers or paints, we recommend putting a blank sheet of paper or cardboard behind each image, so that your colors don't run onto the next image.

1. Light Green
2. Bright Orange
3. Orange
4. Dark Yellow
5. Dark Orange
6. Dark Red
7. Beige
8. Red
9. Deep Green
10. Navy Blue
11. Baby Blue
12. Light Pink
13. Hot Pink
14. Blue
15. Light Violet
16. Green
17. Yellow

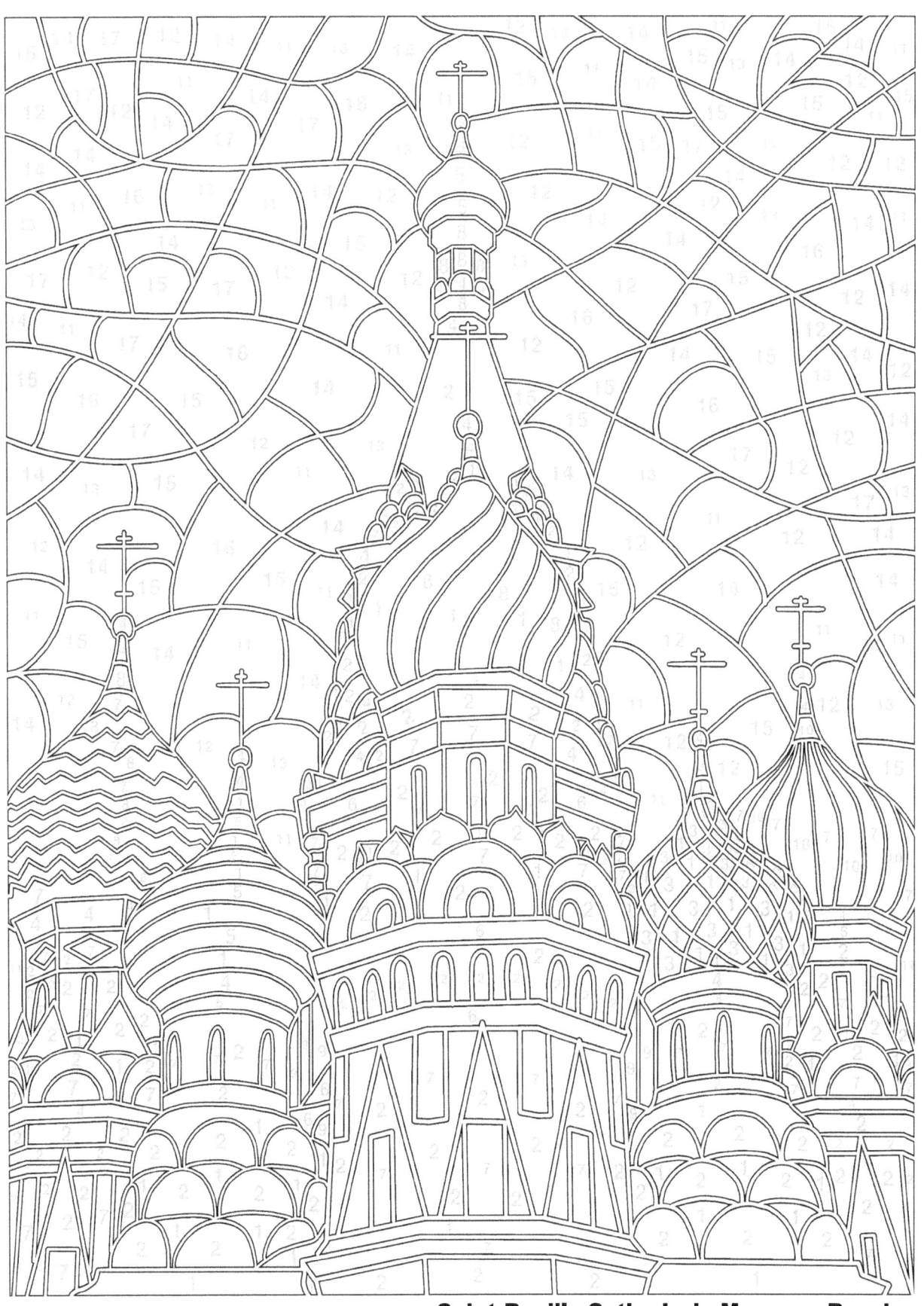

Saint Basil's Cathedral - Moscow, Russia

1. Medium Gray

2. Dark Gray

3. Gray

4. Purple

5. Light Gray

6. Green

7. Neon Green

8. Army Green

9. Brown

10. Light Orange

11. Beige

12. Light Blue

13. Baby Blue

14. Navy Blue

15. Light Pink

16. Yellow

17. Hot Pink

18. Medium Blue

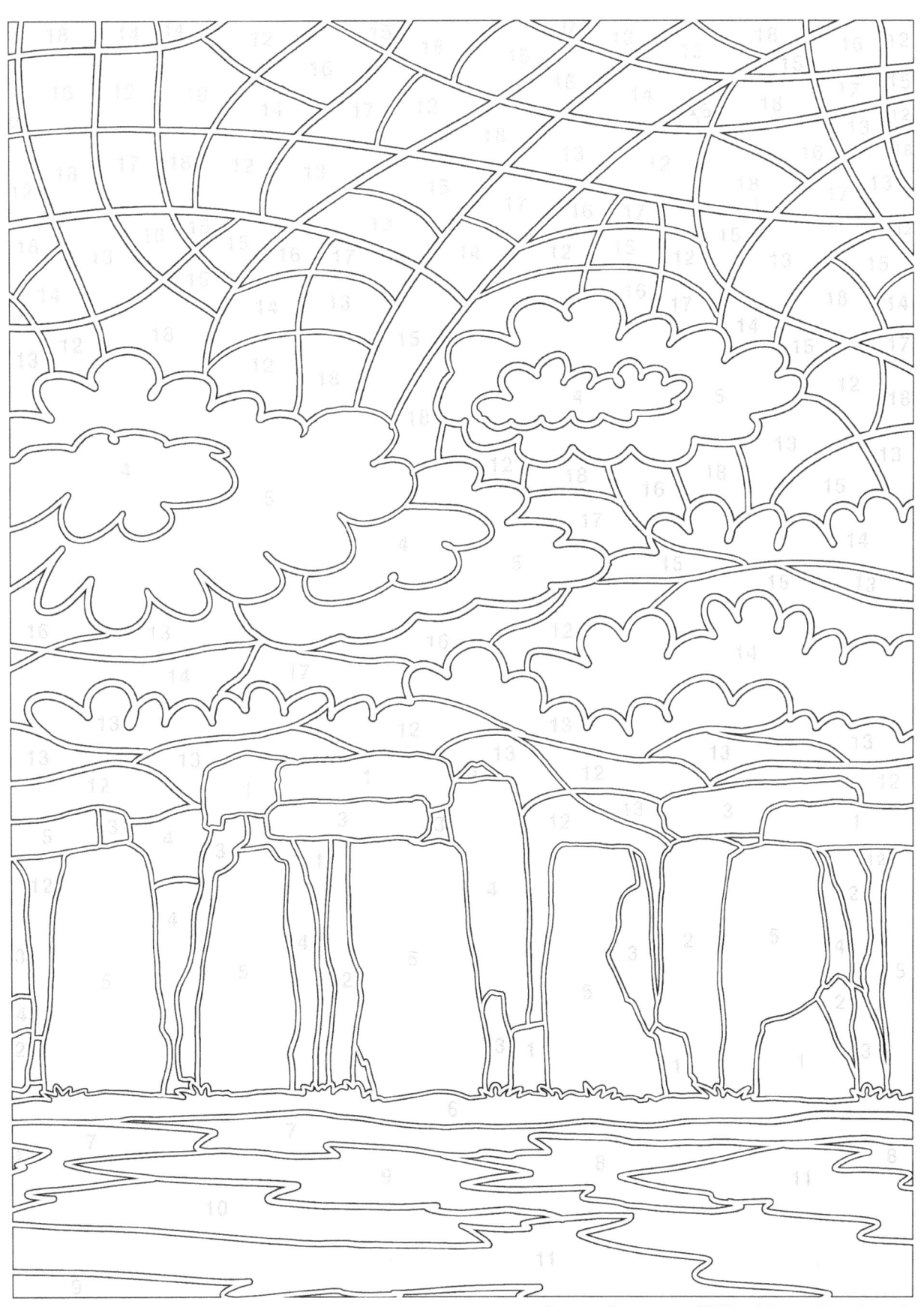

Stonehenge - Wiltshire, England

1. Dark Brown

2. Light Red

3. Beige

4. Medium Red

5. Light Yellow

6. Light Green

7. Medium Green

8. Deep Green

9. Orange

10. Army Green

11. Grey Purple

12. Dark Gray

13. Medium Gray

14. Light Gray

15. Gray

16. Light Brown

17. Medium Brown

18. Baby Blue

19. Blue

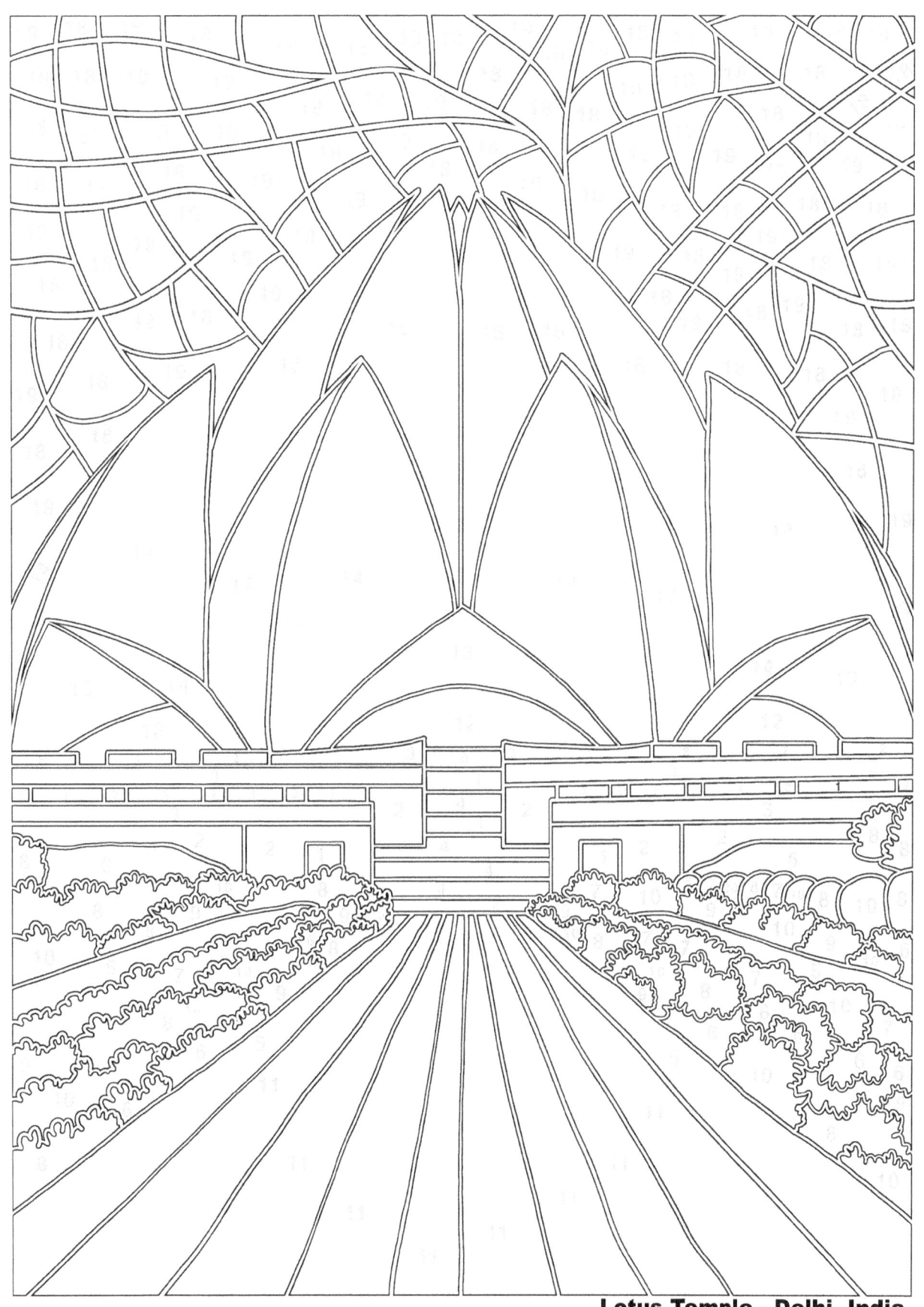

Lotus Temple - Delhi, India

1. Dark Brown

2. Orange

3. Light Yellow

4. Beige

5. Green

6. Deep Green

7. Brown

8. Light Gray

9. Medium Brown

10. Sky Blue

11. Blue

12. Light Green

13. Army Green

14. Navy Blue

15. Pink

16. Baby Blue

17. Violet

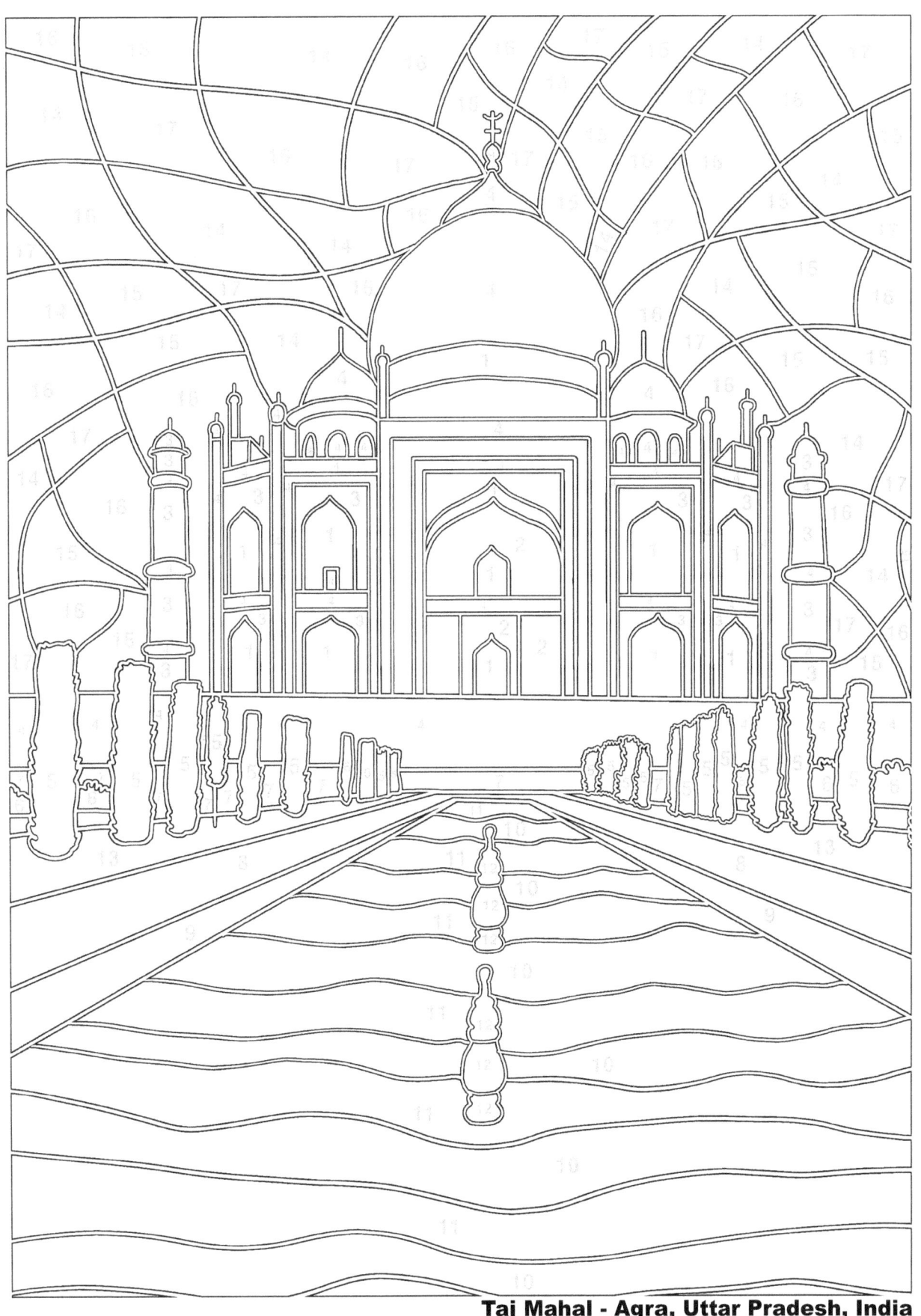

Taj Mahal - Agra, Uttar Pradesh, India

1. Light Gray

2. Gray

3. Purple

4. Dark Gray

5. Dark Brown

6. Medium Gray

7. Light Brown

8. Green

9. Neon Green

10. Deep Green

11. Light Green

12. Light Yellow

13. Medium Green

14. Blue

15. Beige

16. Violet

17. Navy Blue

18. Yellow

19. Hot Pink

20. Sky Blue

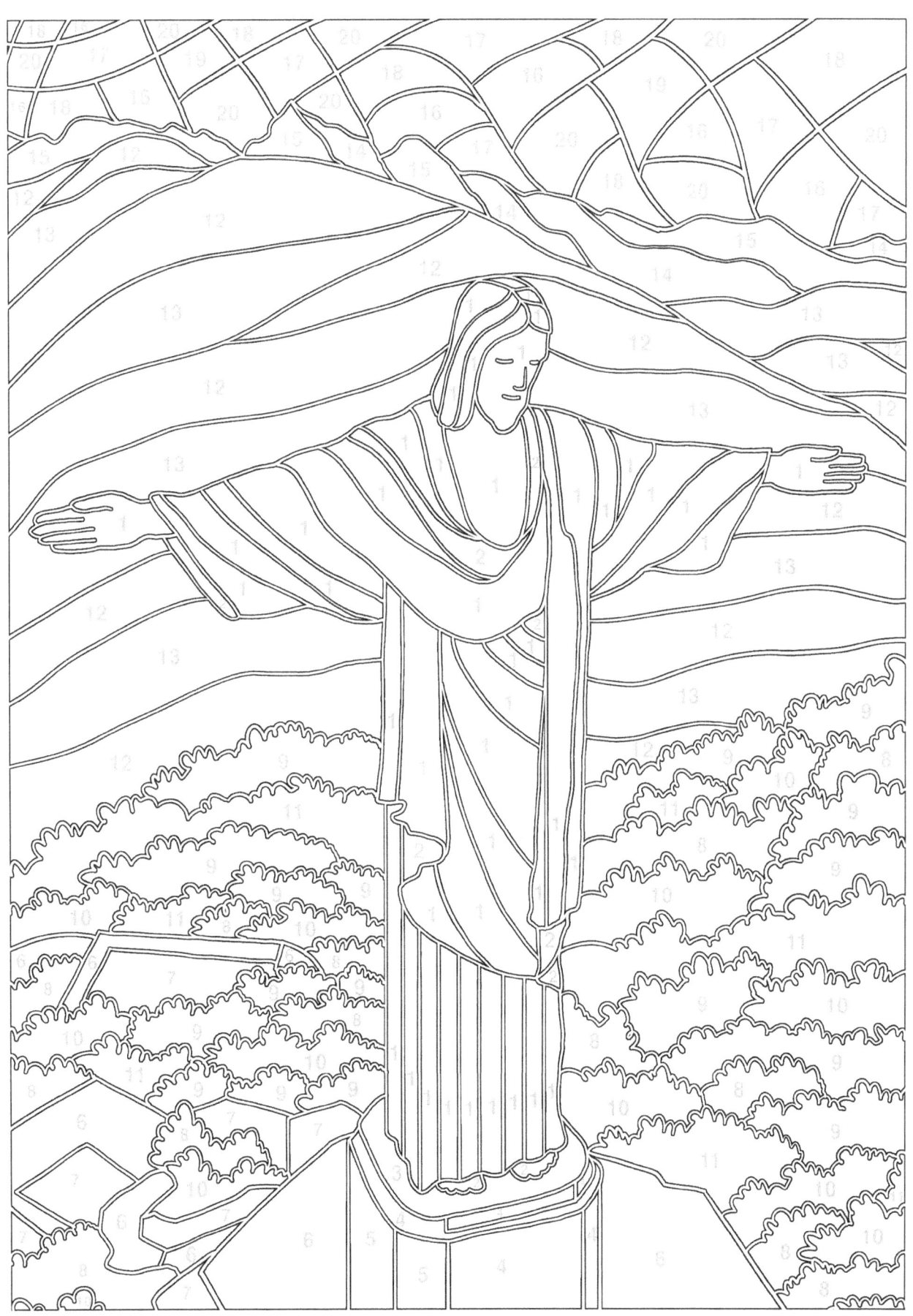

Christ the Redeemer - Rio de Janeiro, Brazil

1. Light Green
2. Medium Green
3. Deep Green
4. Army Green
5. Brown
6. Light Brown
7. Dark Brown
8. Yellow
9. Blue
10. Violet
11. Orange
12. Beige
13. Pink
14. Dark Orange
15. Navy Blue
16. Neon Green
17. Baby Blue

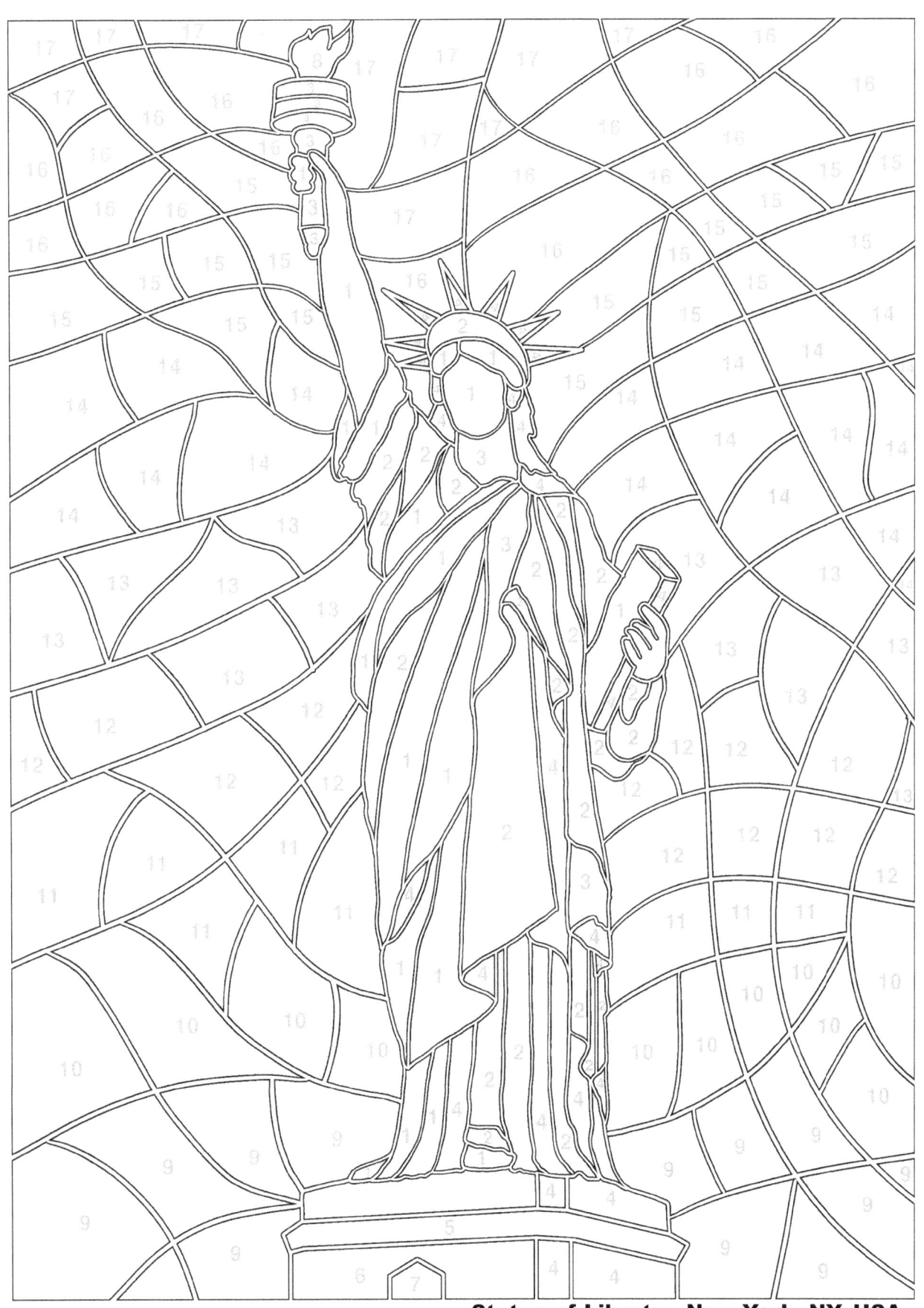

Statue of Liberty - New York, NY, USA

1. Light Gray

2. Dark Gray

3. Medium Gray

4. Light Blue

5. Gray

6. Light Brown

7. Brown

8. Dark Brown

9. Deep Green

10. Light Green

11. Neon Green

12. Light Yellow

13. Blue

14. Light Blue

15. Light Pink

16. Orange

17. Light Violet

18. Yellow

19. Sky Blue

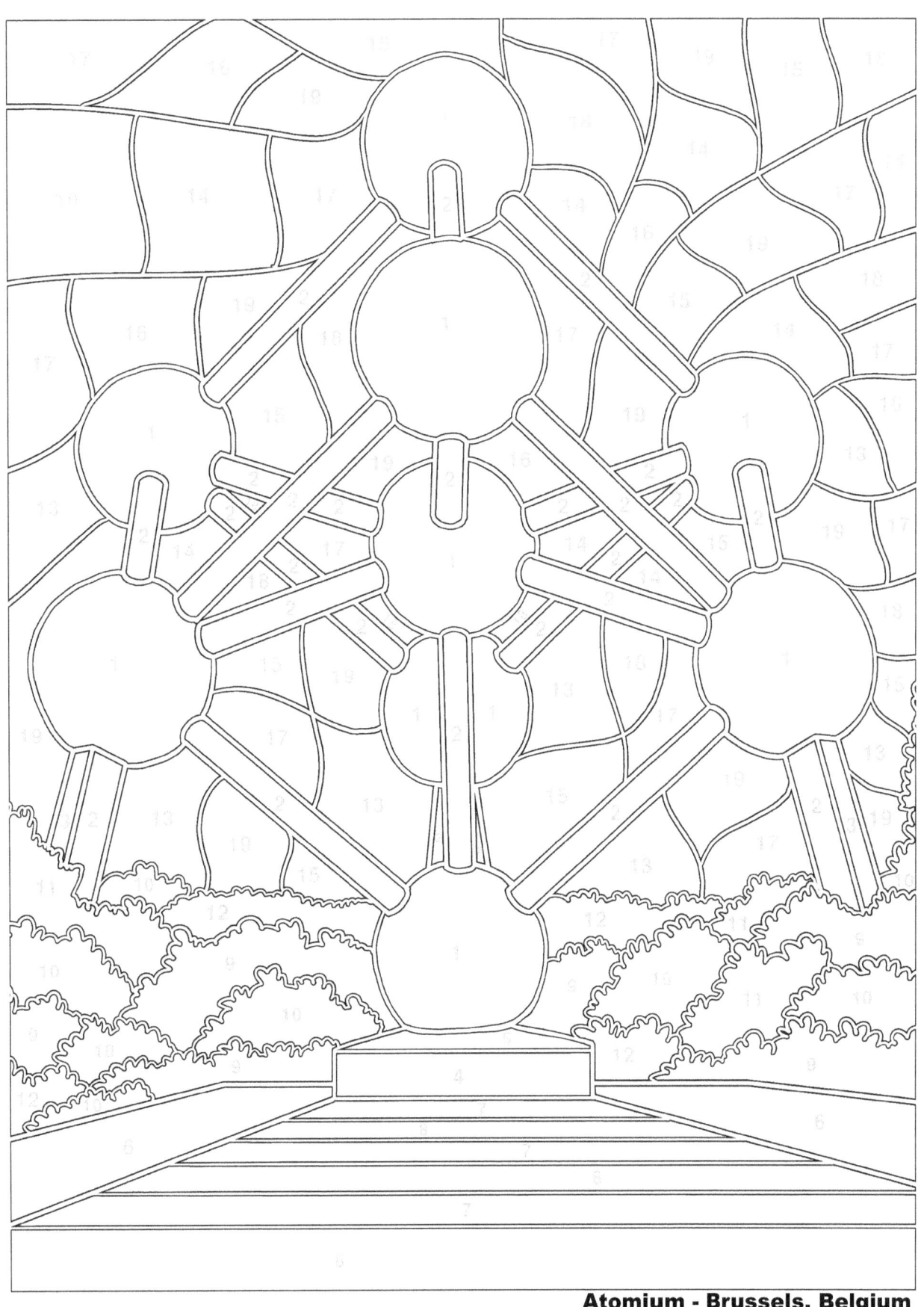

Atomium - Brussels, Belgium

1. Brown

2. Dark Brown

3. Beige

4. Light Gray

5. Light Brown

6. Medium Brown

7. Gray

8. Beige

9. Deep Green

10. Green

11. Neon Green

12. Sky Blue

13. Light Violet

14. Light Pink

15. Yellow

16. Navy Blue

17. Baby blue

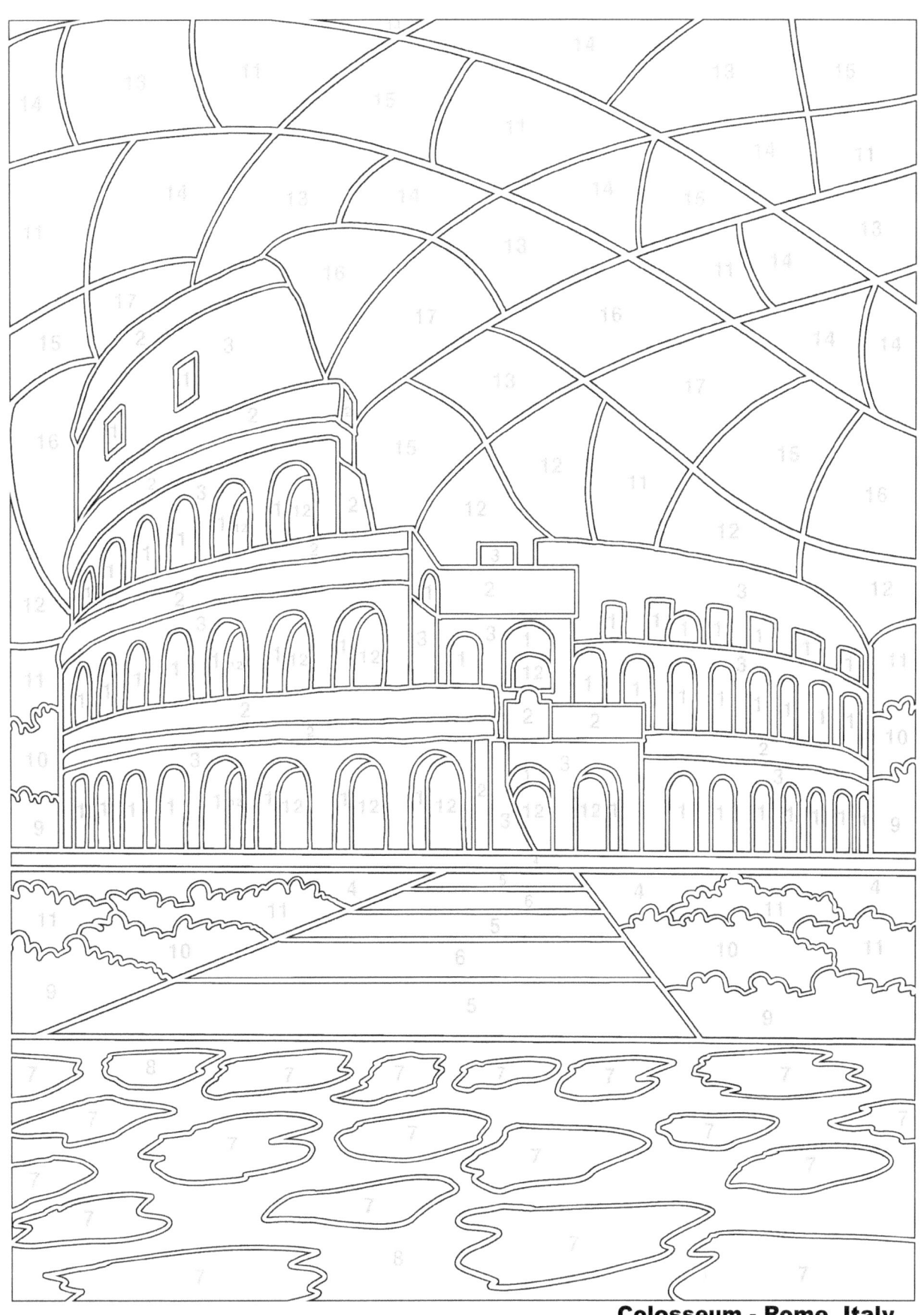

Colosseum - Rome, Italy

1. Gray
2. Light Gray
3. Dark Gray
4. Medium Gray
5. Dark Violet
6. Navy Blue
7. Medium Blue
8. Blue
9. Baby Blue
10. Orange
11. Dark Blue
12. Light Violet
13. Light Green
14. Army Green
15. Yellow
16. Light Pink
17. Sky Blue
18. Light Brown
19. Medium Brown

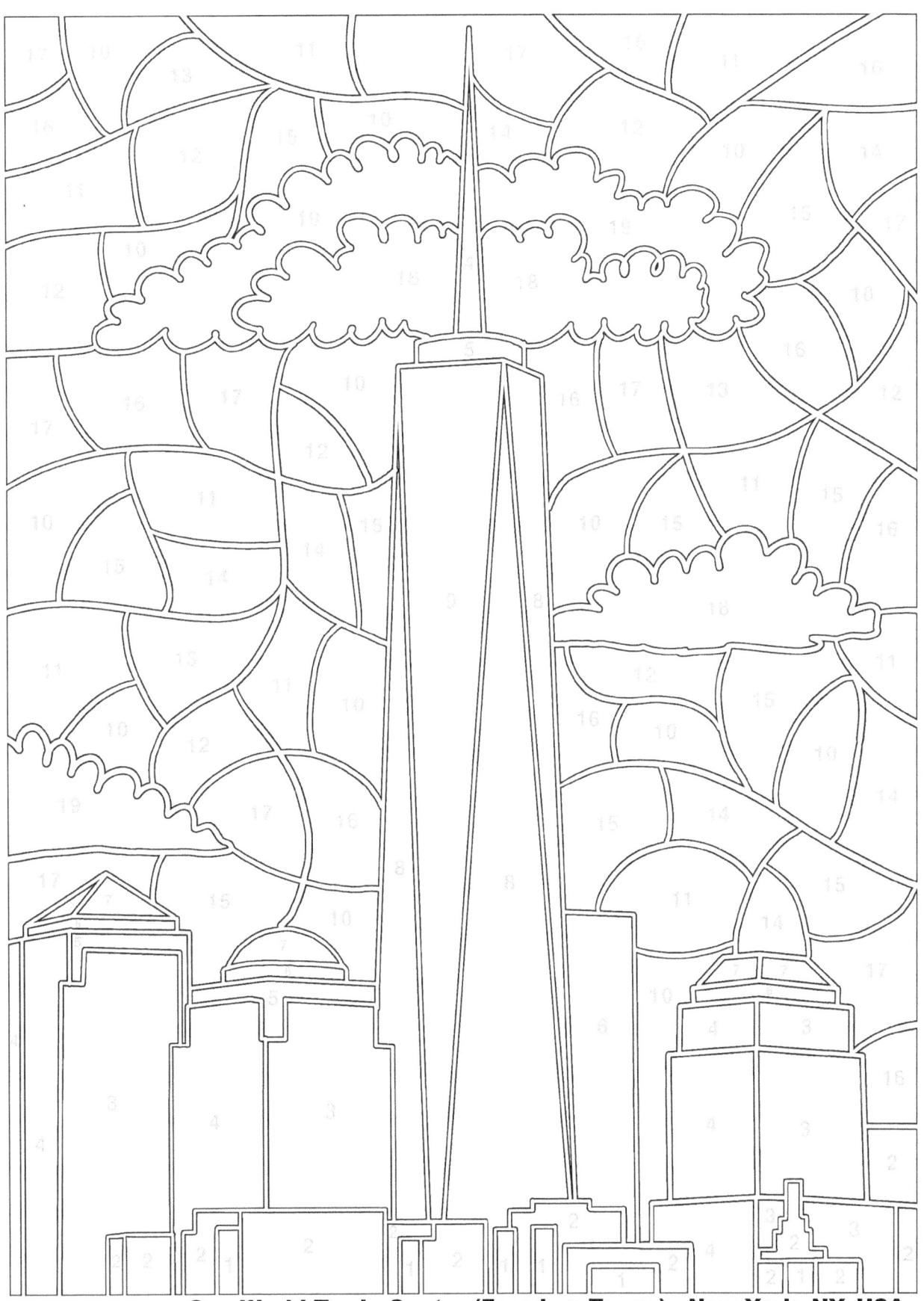

One World Trade Center (Freedom Tower) - New York, NY, USA

1. Light Brown
2. Medium Brown
3. Dark Brown
4. Gray
5. Dark Gray
6. Yellow
7. Orange
8. Brown
9. Soft Violet
10. Green
11. Deep Green
12. Light Green
13. Medium Gray
14. Light Gray
15. Navy Blue

16. Sky Blue
17. Light Pink
18. Dark Yellow

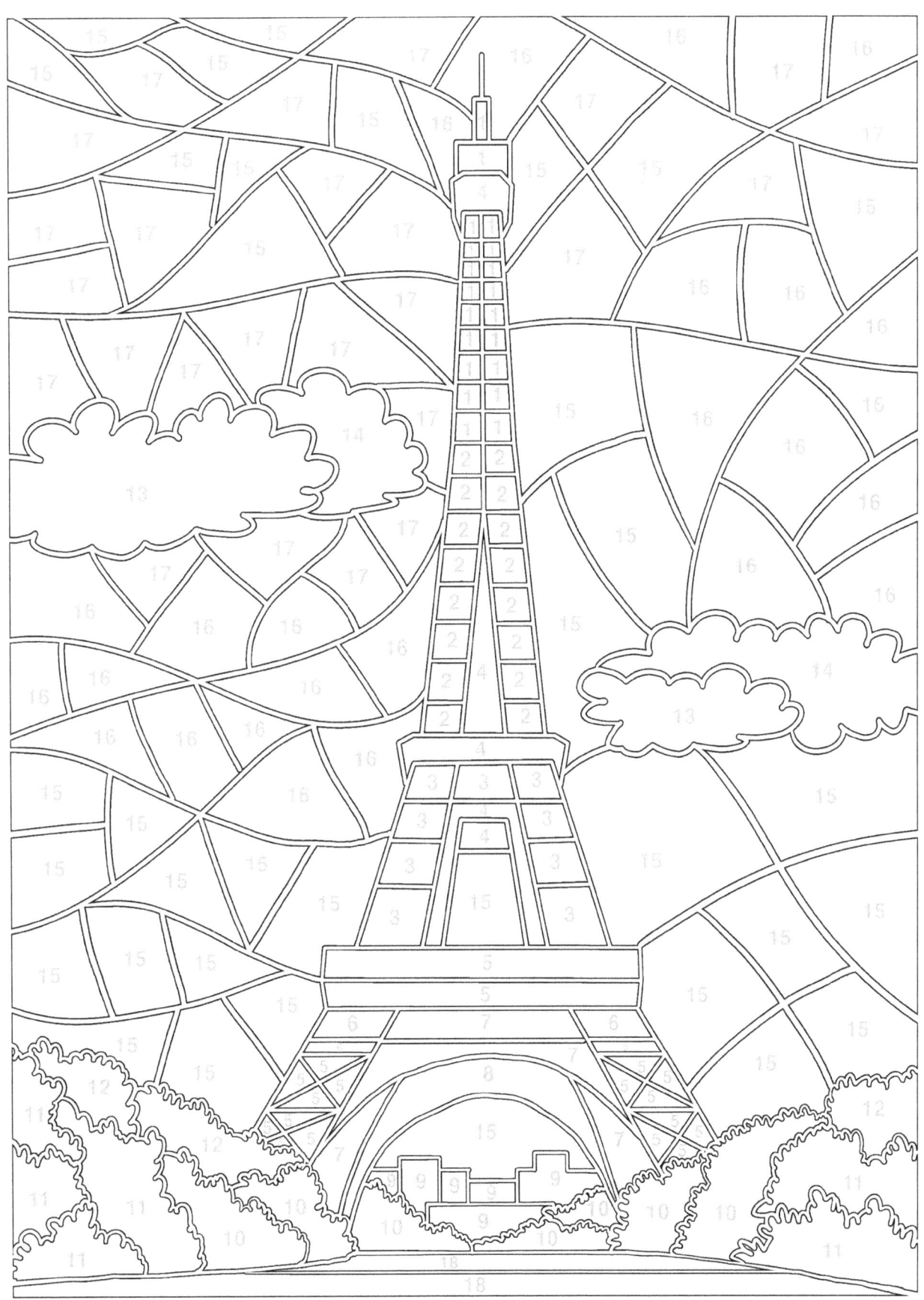

Eiffel Tower - Paris, France

1. Gray

2. Soft Violet

3. Medium Violet

4. Dark Violet

5. Brown

6. Green

7. Orange

8. Dark Brown

9. Light Gray

10. Light Blue

11. Navy Blue

12. Light Pink

13. Sky Blue

14. Yellow

15. Navy Blue

16. Light Red

17. Dark Orange

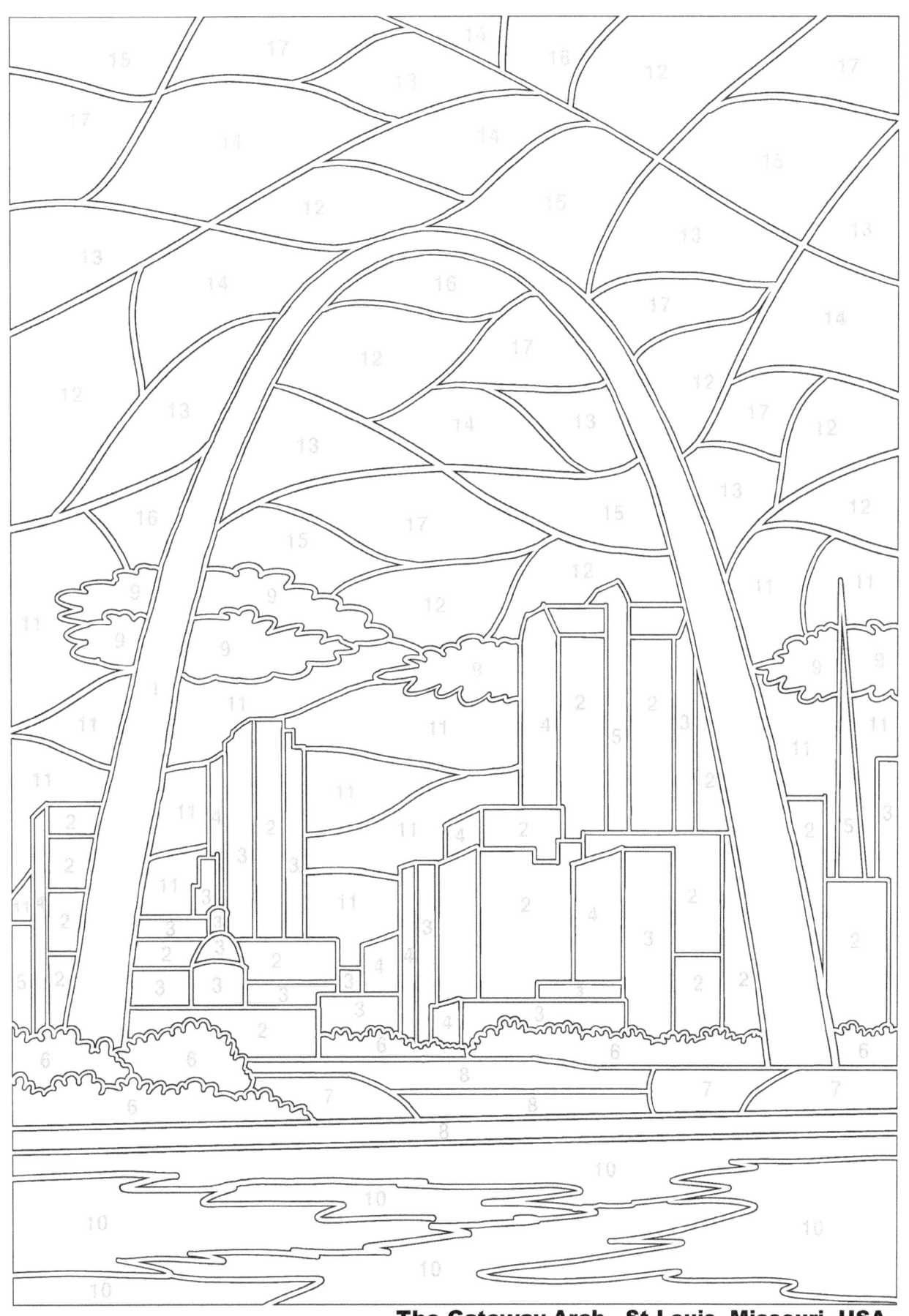

The Gateway Arch - St Louis, Missouri, USA

1. Gray
2. Medium Gray
3. Dark Gray
4. Dark Violet
5. Violet
6. Light Violet
7. Green
8. Dark Brown
9. Light Brown
10. Light Blue
11. Light Gray
12. Beige
13. Sky Blue
14. Light Pink
15. Navy Blue
16. Yellow
17. Orange

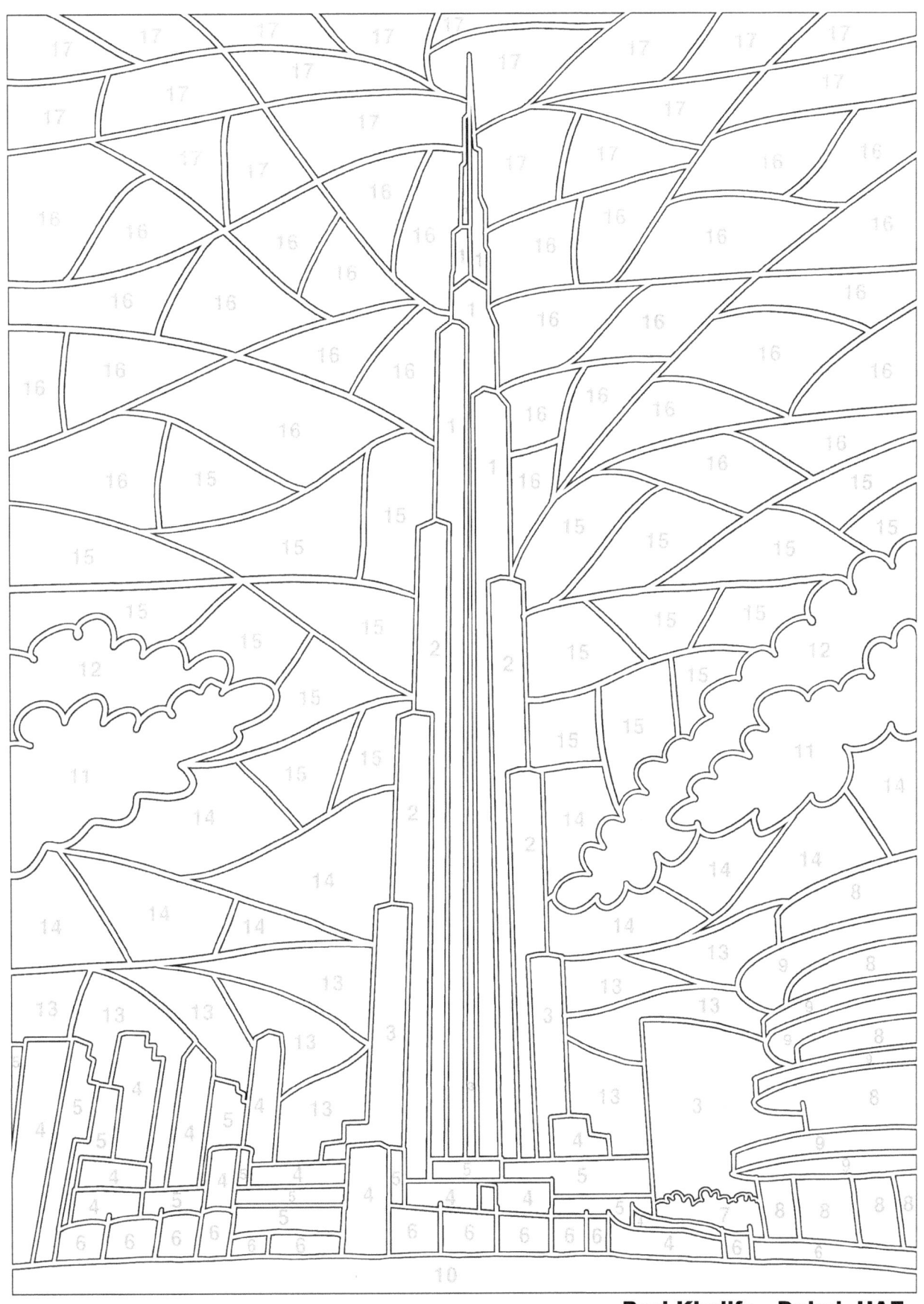

Burj Khalifa - Dubai, UAE

1. Gray

2. Medium Violet

3. Light Gray

4. Soft Violet

5. Violet

6. Dark Violet

7. Light Violet

8. Light Brown

9. Dark Brown

10. Light Blue

11. Deep Blue

12. Medium Blue

13. Sky Blue

14. Light Pink

15. Navy Blue

16. Yellow

17. Orange

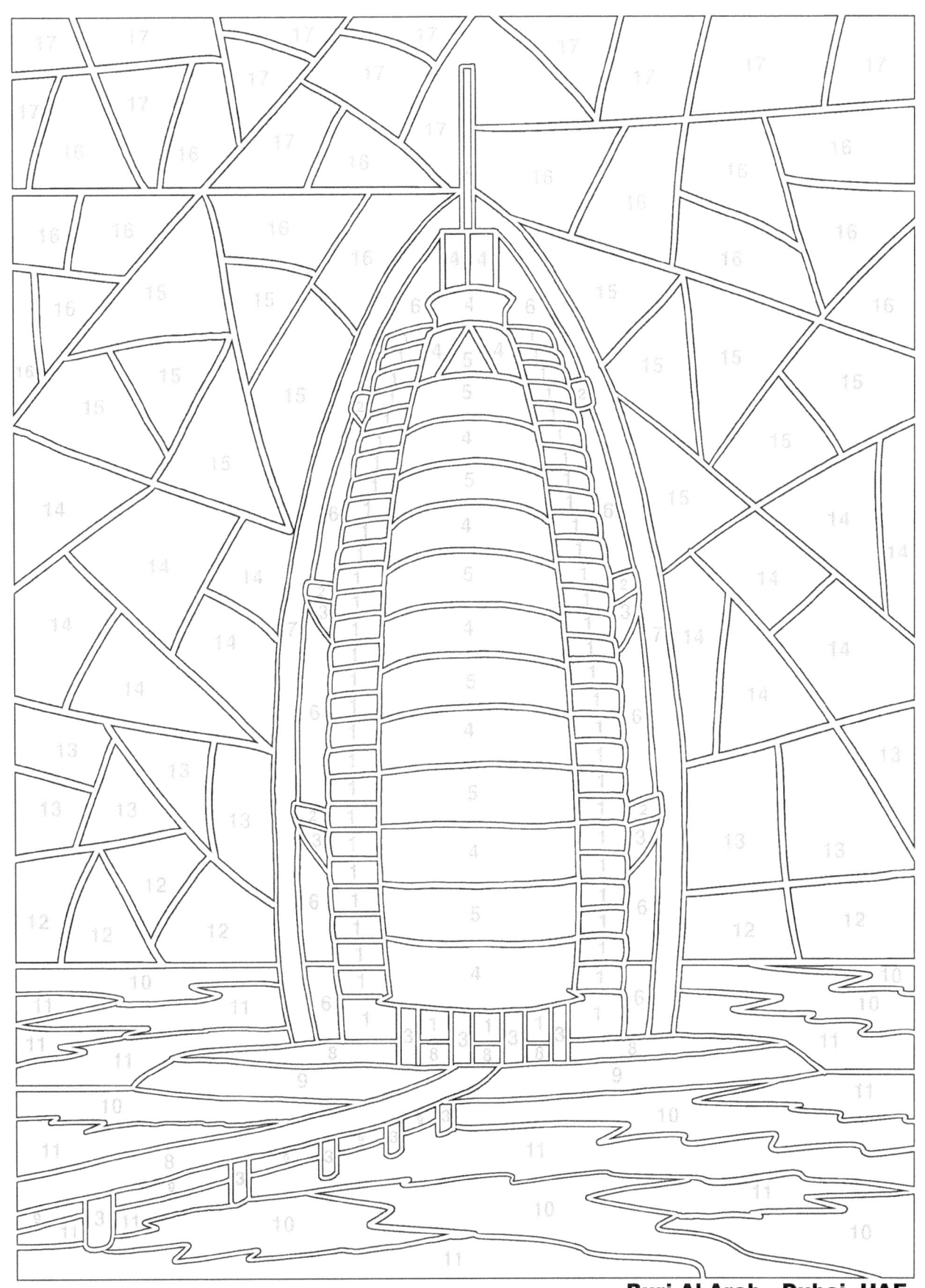

Burj Al Arab - Dubai, UAE

1. Light Brown
2. Brown
3. Dark Brown
4. Yellow
5. Medium Brown
6. Orange
7. Dark Orange
8. Medium Orange
9. Medium Gray
10. Light Gray
11. Dark Gray
12. Medium Blue
13. Sky Blue
14. Light Pink
15. Navy Blue
16. Violet
17. Light Orange

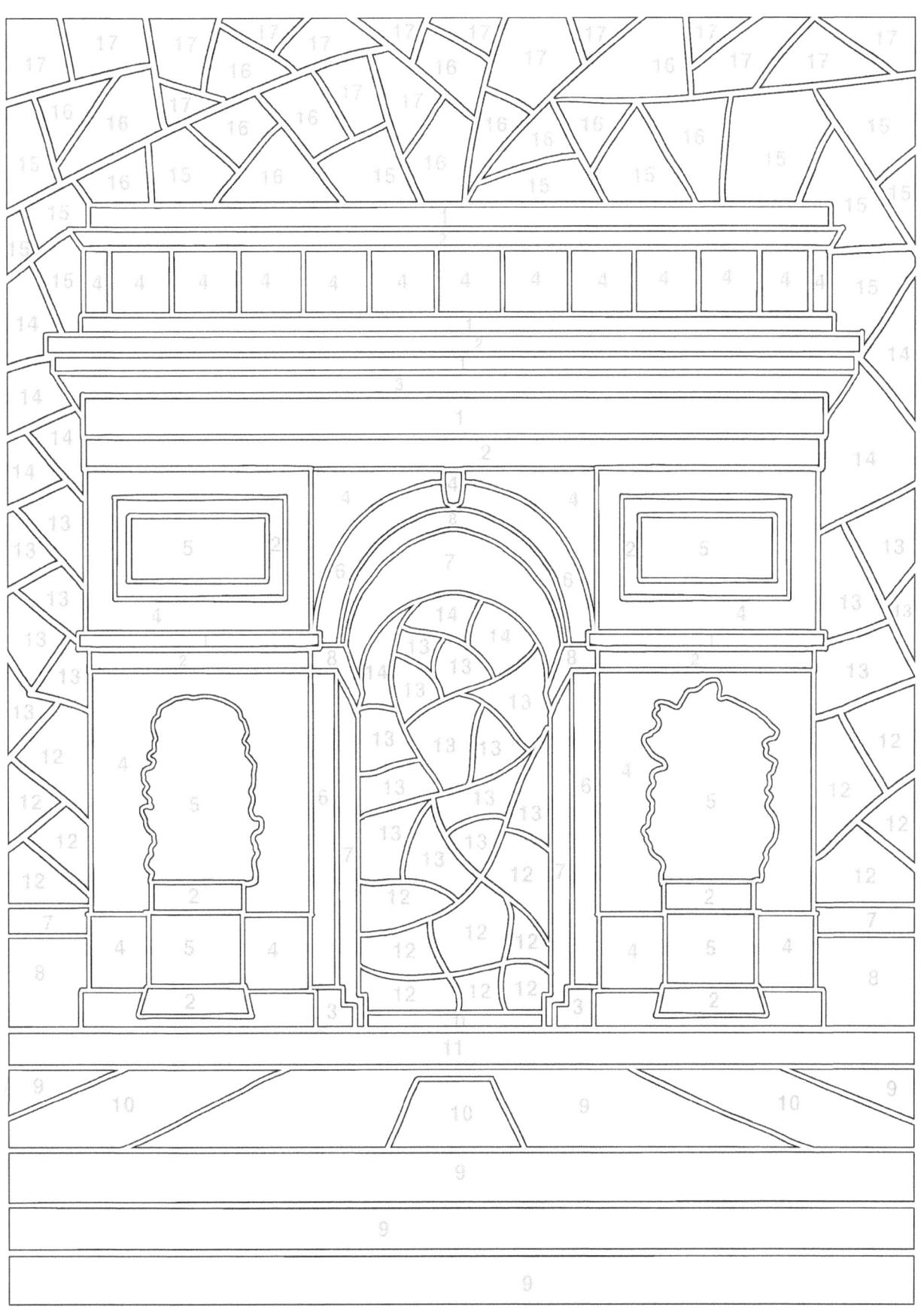

Arc de Triomphe - Paris, France

1. Brown
2. Dark Brown
3. Medium Brown
4. Dark Orange
5. Orange
6. Yellow
7. Light Orange
8. Medium Orange
9. Light Browen
10. Light Gray
11. Dark Gray
12. Medium Gray
13. Gray
14. Blue
15. Sky Blue
16. Light Pink
17. Light Violet

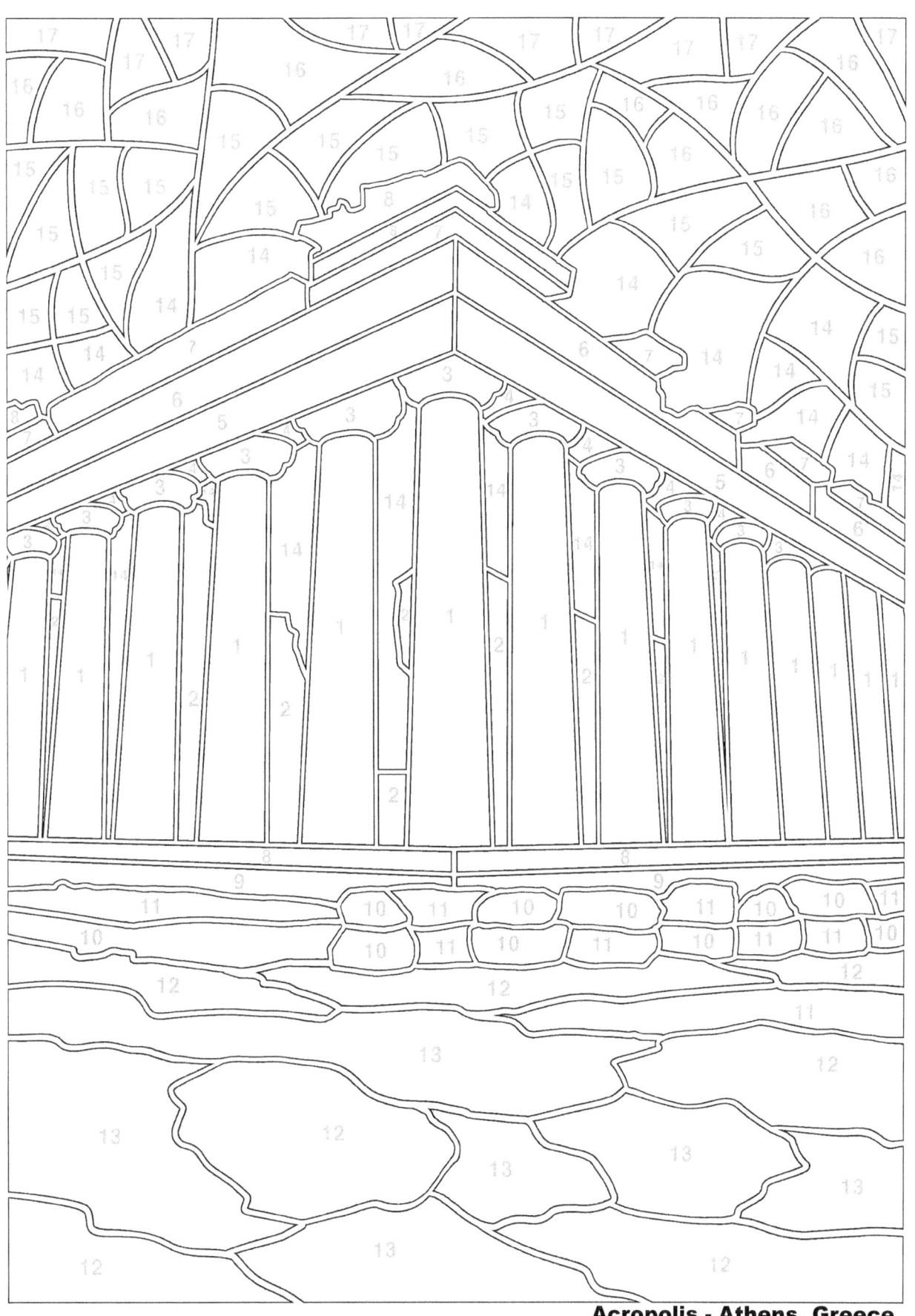

Acropolis - Athens, Greece

1. Light Brown
2. Brown
3. Dark Brown
4. Medium Brown
5. Yellow
6. Dark Orange
7. Dark Green
8. Green
9. Light Green
10. Medium Green
11. Army Green
12. Gray
13. Light Gray
14. Sky Blue
15. Violet
16. Light Pink
17. Blue

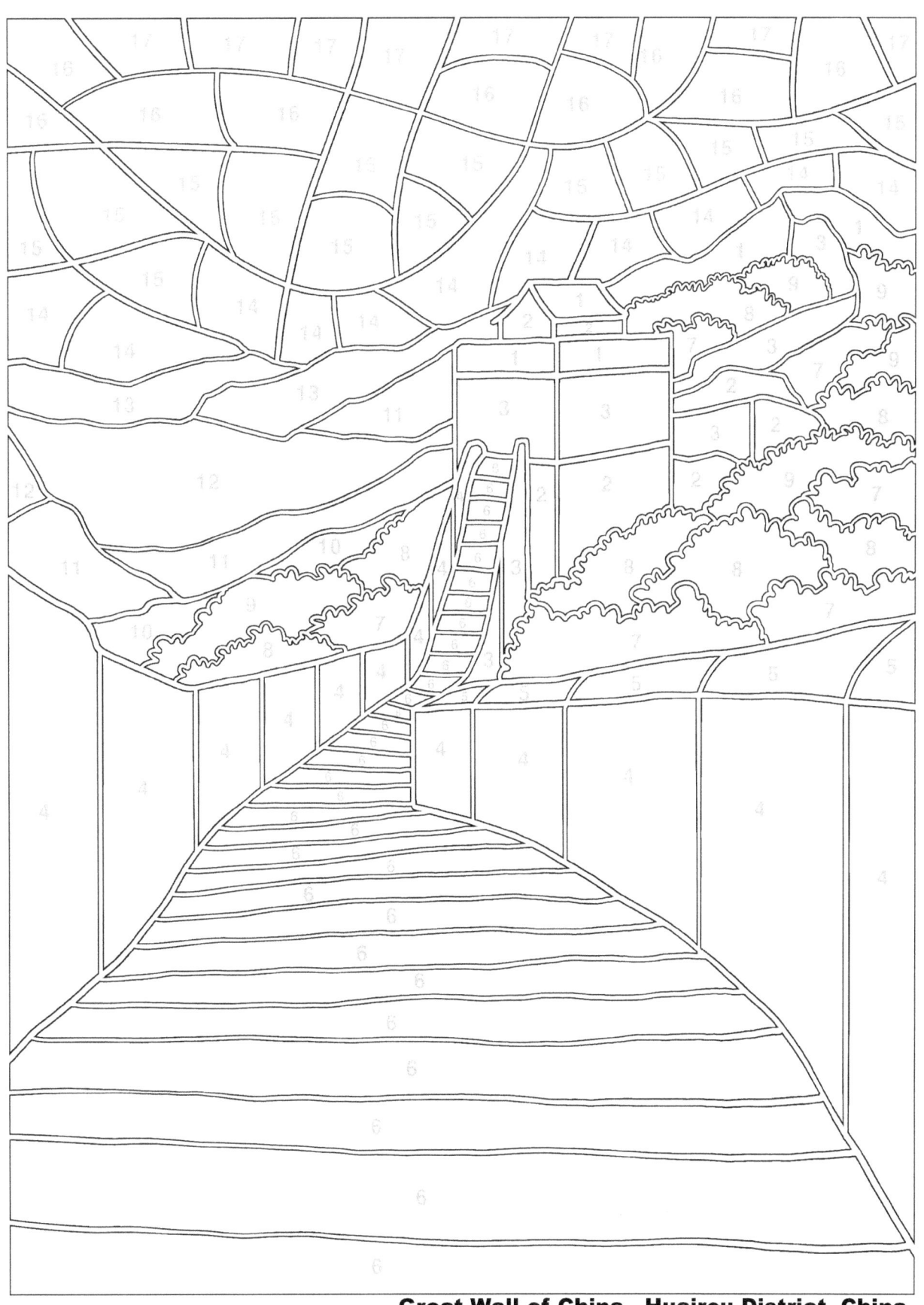

Great Wall of China - Huairou District, China

1. Gray
2. Dark Gray
3. Brown
4. Red
5. Medium Gray
6. Medium Brown
7. Light Gray
8. Dark Violet
9. Medium Violet
10. Violet
11. Light Violet
12. Green
13. Light Green
14. Blue
15. Light Orange
16. Sky Blue
17. Light Pink

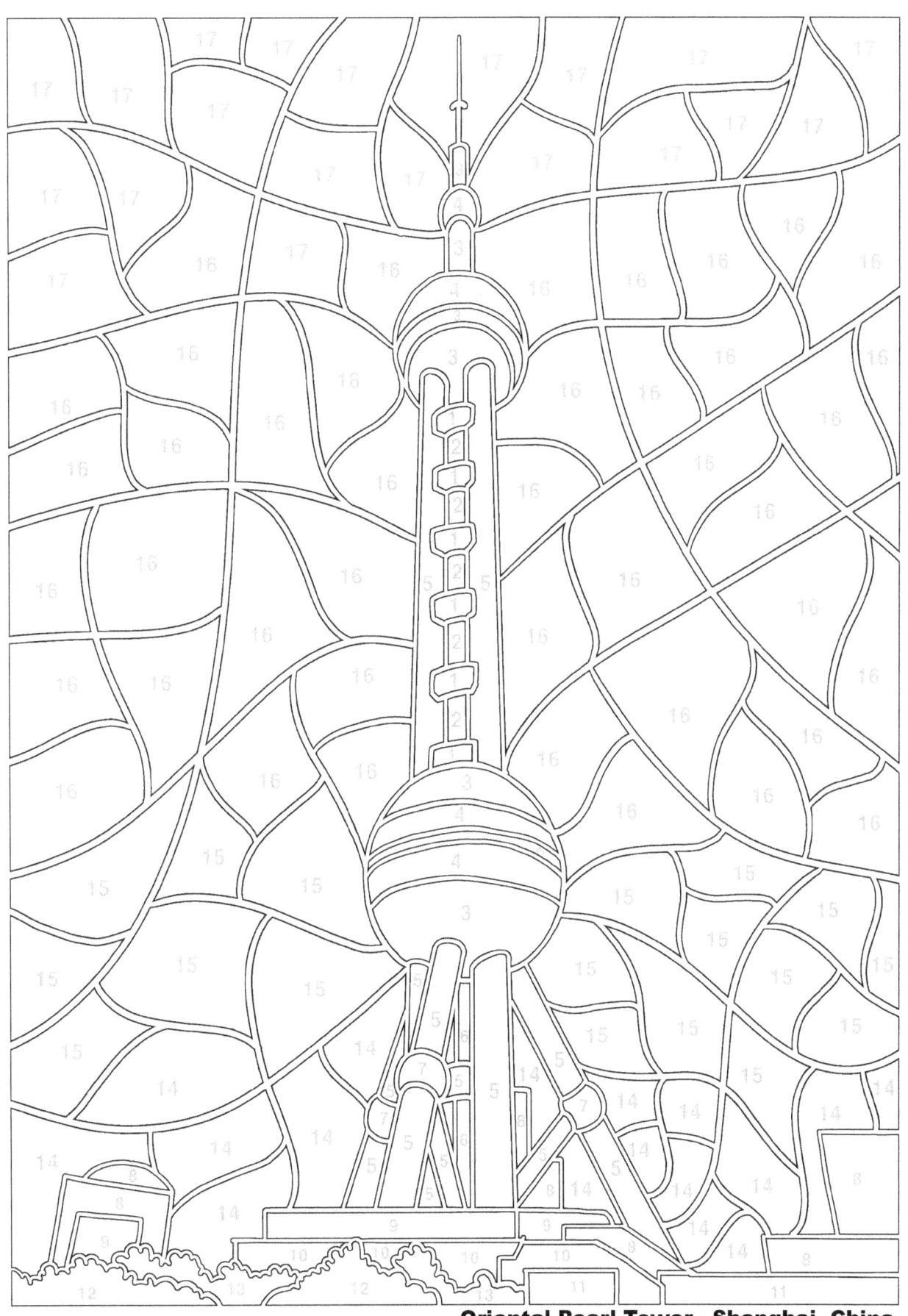

Oriental Pearl Tower - Shanghai, China

1. Black
2. Iron Gray
3. Deep Brown
4. Gray
5. Medium Gray
6. Light Gray
7. Silver Gray
8. Deep Gray
9. Light Yellow
10. Beige
11. Medium Green
12. Light blue green
13. Light Green
14. Olive Green
15. Sky Blue
16. Light pink
17. Pink
18. Medium Blue
19. Light purple
20. Royal Blue

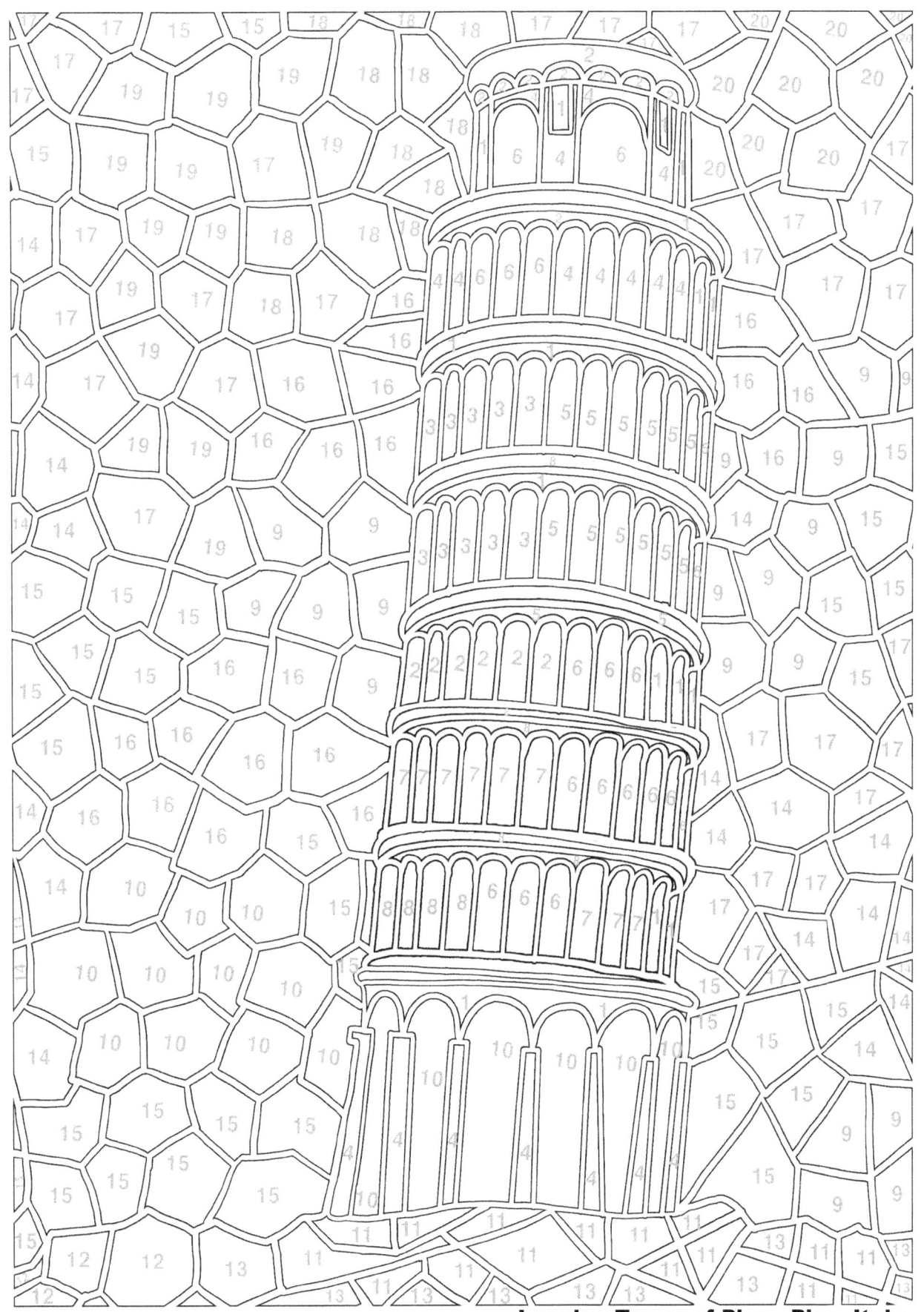

Leaning Tower of Pisa - Pisa, Italy

1. Black
2. Reddish Brown
3. Dark Brown
4. Light Brown
5. Golden Yellow
6. Yellow Ocher
7. Bronze
8. Sand Yellow
9. Light Yellow
10. Beige
11. Mustard Yellow
12. Dark Yellow
13. Sky Blue
14. Medium Blue
15. Light purple
16. Light pink
17. Pink
18. Royal Blue
19. Pale Turquoise
20. Violet

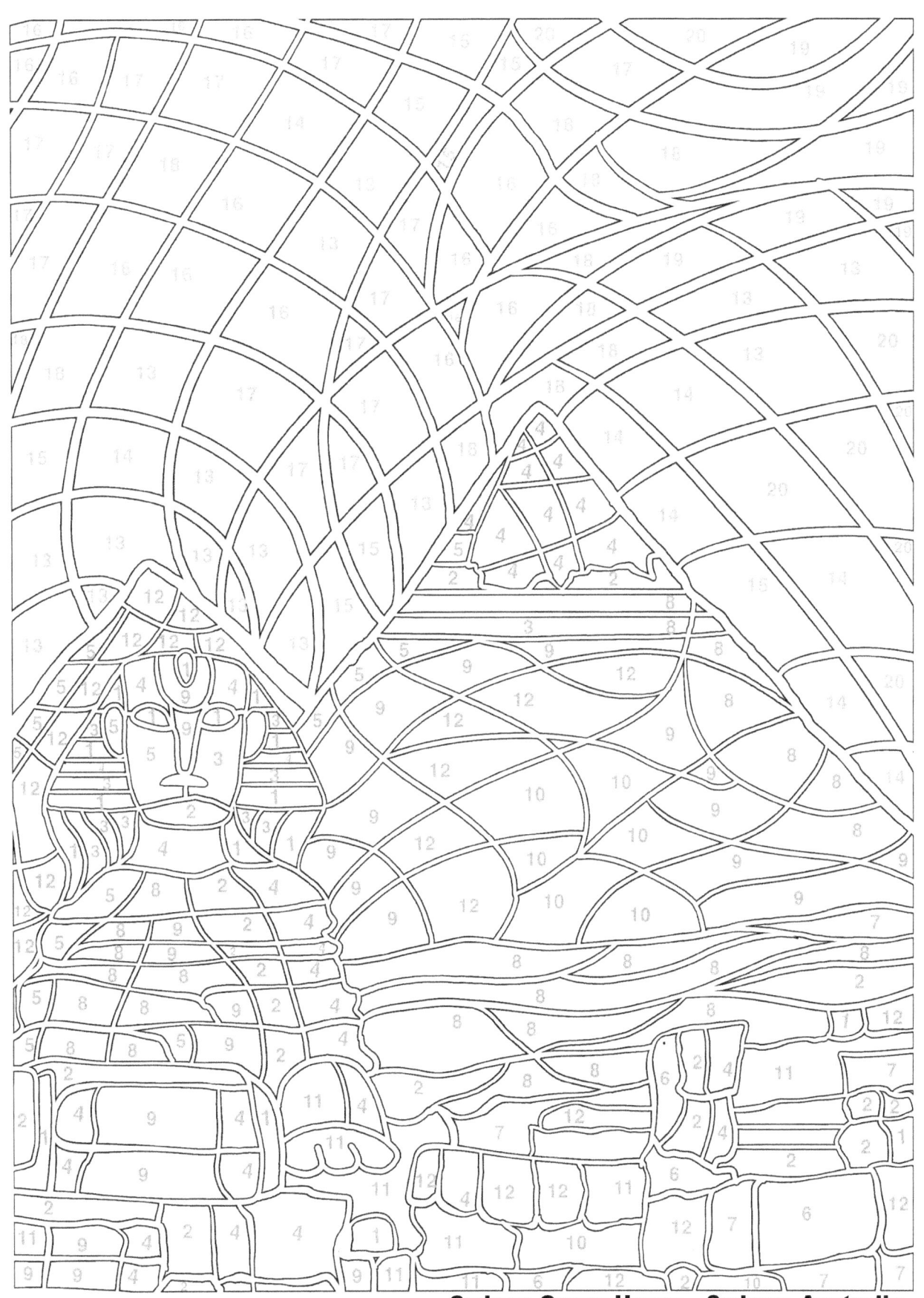

Sydney Opera House - Sydney, Australia

1. Black

2. Iron Gray

3. Dark Brown

4. Gray

5. Medium Gray

6. Beige

7. Sand

8. Slate Gray

9. Ocean Blue

10. Aqua Blue

11. Royal Blue

12. Turquoise Blue

13. Sky Blue

14. Light purple

15. Light Yellow

16. Light pink

17. Pink

18. Medium Blue

19. Pale Turquoise

20. Navy Blue

21. Violet

22. Lemon Yellow

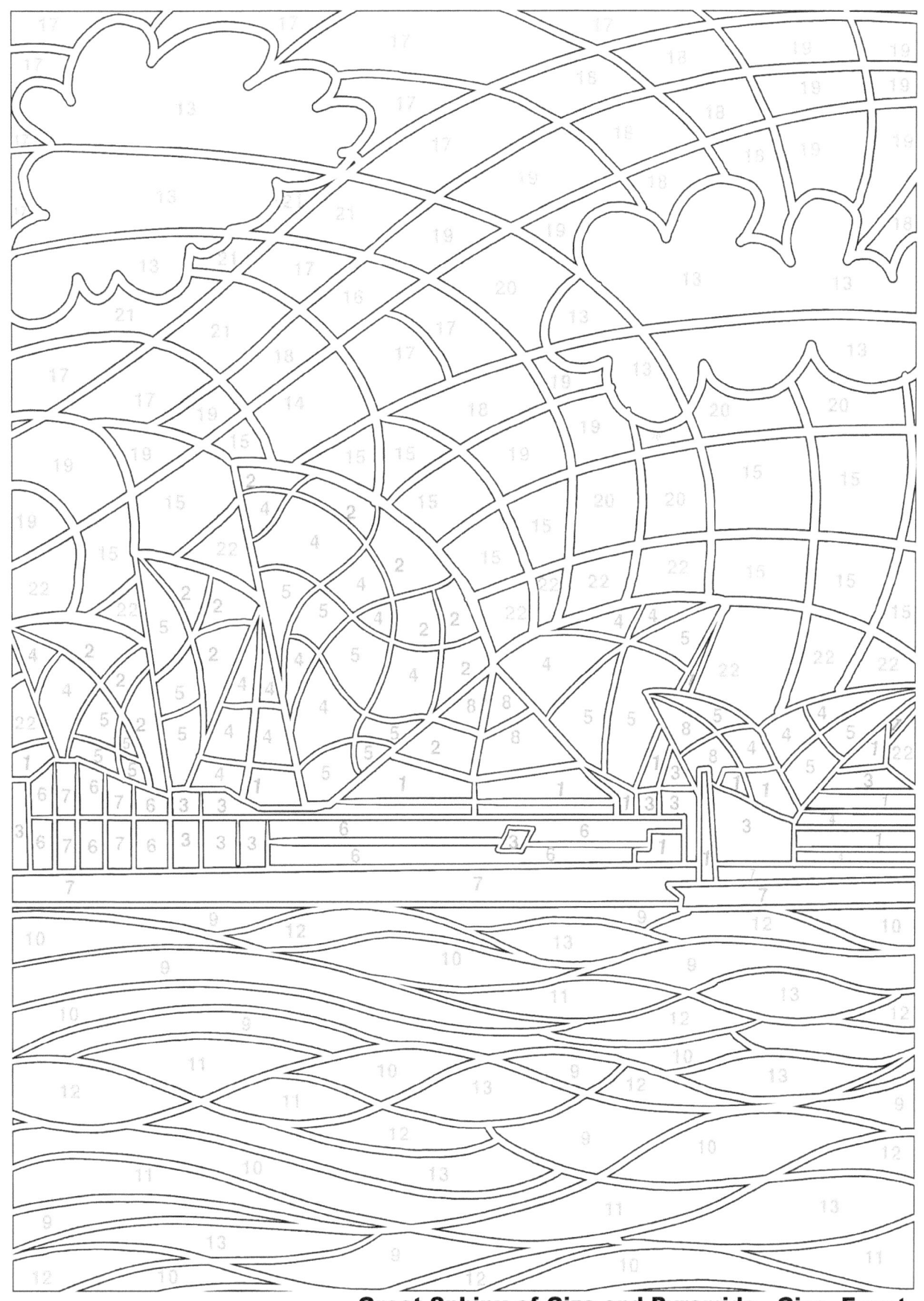

Great Sphinx of Giza and Pyramids - Giza, Egypt

ENJOY BONUS
IMAGES FROM SOME
OF OUR
OTHER FUN
COLOR BY NUMBER
BOOKS!

FIND ALL OF OUR
BOOKS
ON AMAZON

Easy Design
Adult Color By Number
Jumbo Coloring Book of Large Print
Flowers, Birds, and Butterflies

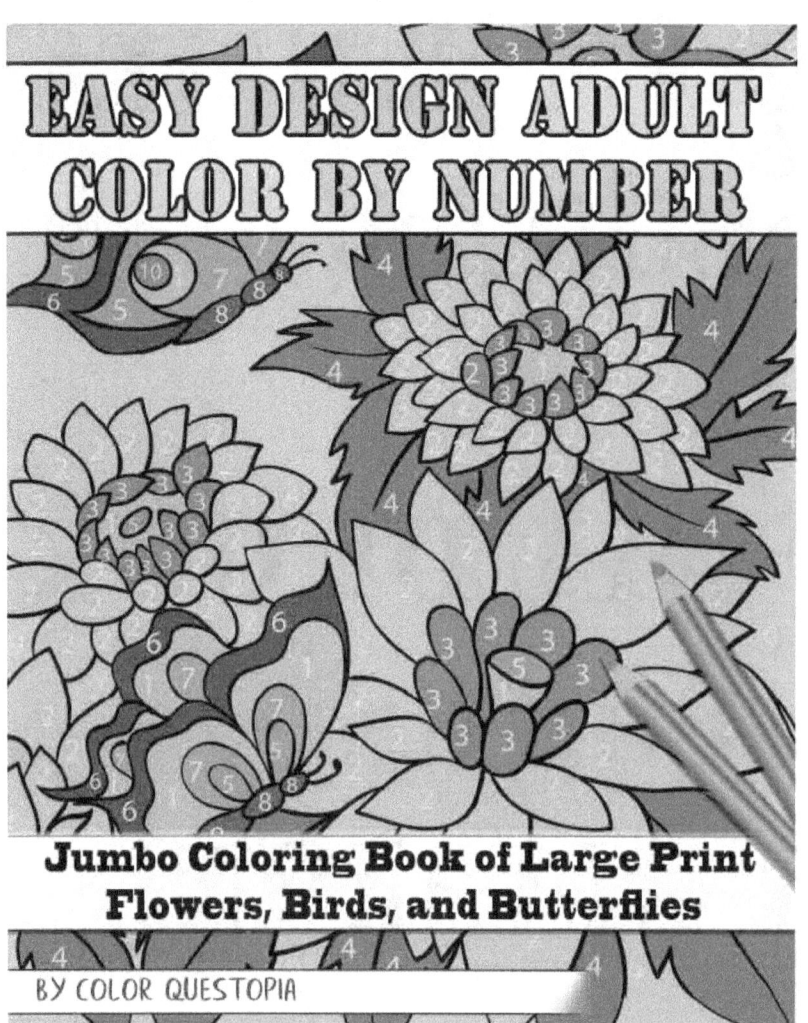

1. Pink   2. Yellow   3. Green   4. Red   5.Orange   6. Dark Blue
7. Brown   8. Sky Blue   9. Purple   10. Light Pink

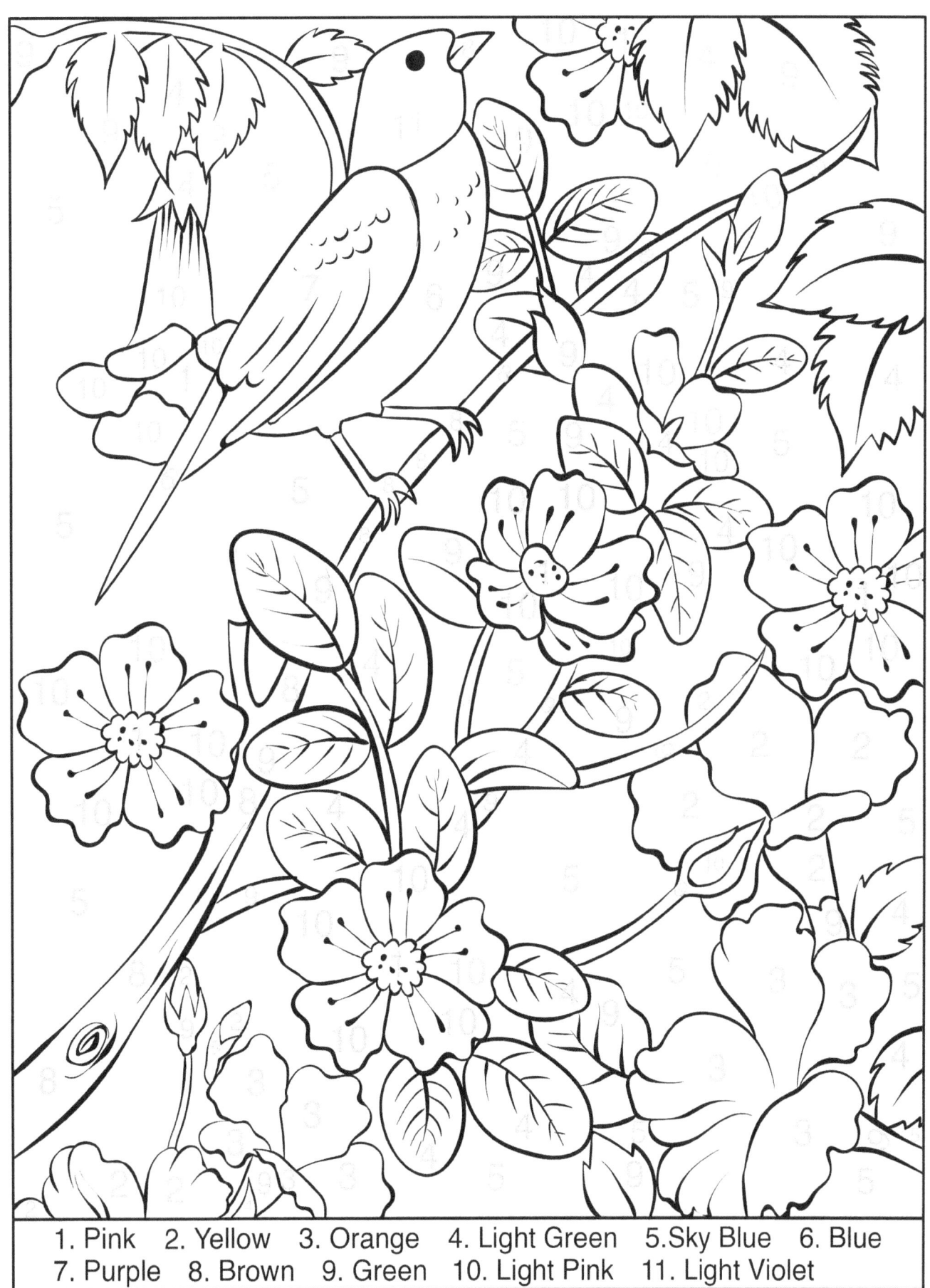

1. Pink   2. Yellow   3. Orange   4. Light Green   5. Sky Blue   6. Blue
7. Purple   8. Brown   9. Green   10. Light Pink   11. Light Violet

Horses Jumbo Adult Coloring Book
Horses and Ponies Grazing and Racing
Color by Number

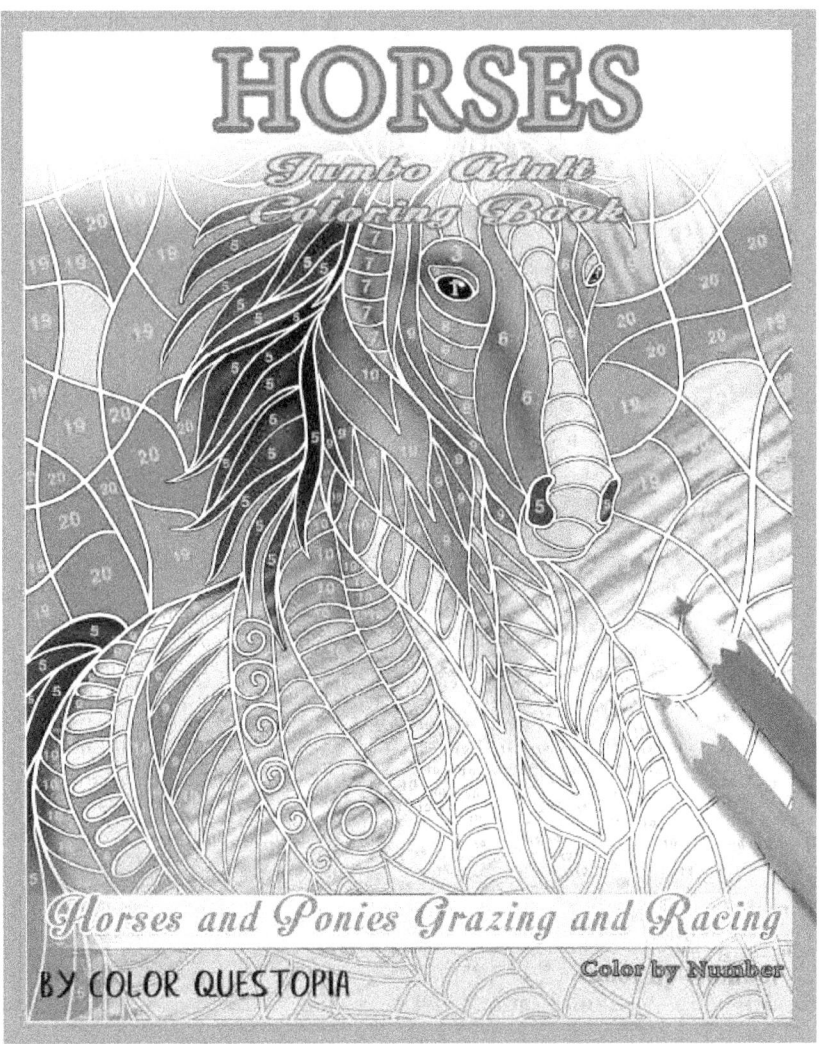

1. Black

2. Light Brown

3. Dark Red

4. Brown

5. Orange

6. Dark Orange

7. Soft Violet

8. Dark Brown

9. Light Red

10. Gray

11. Yellow

12. Dark Red

13. Light Gray

14. Army Green

15. Medium Green

16. Dark Green

17. Violet

18. Blue

19. Pink

20. Neon Green

21. Green

22. Light Green

23. Navy Blue

24. Medium Blue

25. Sky Blue

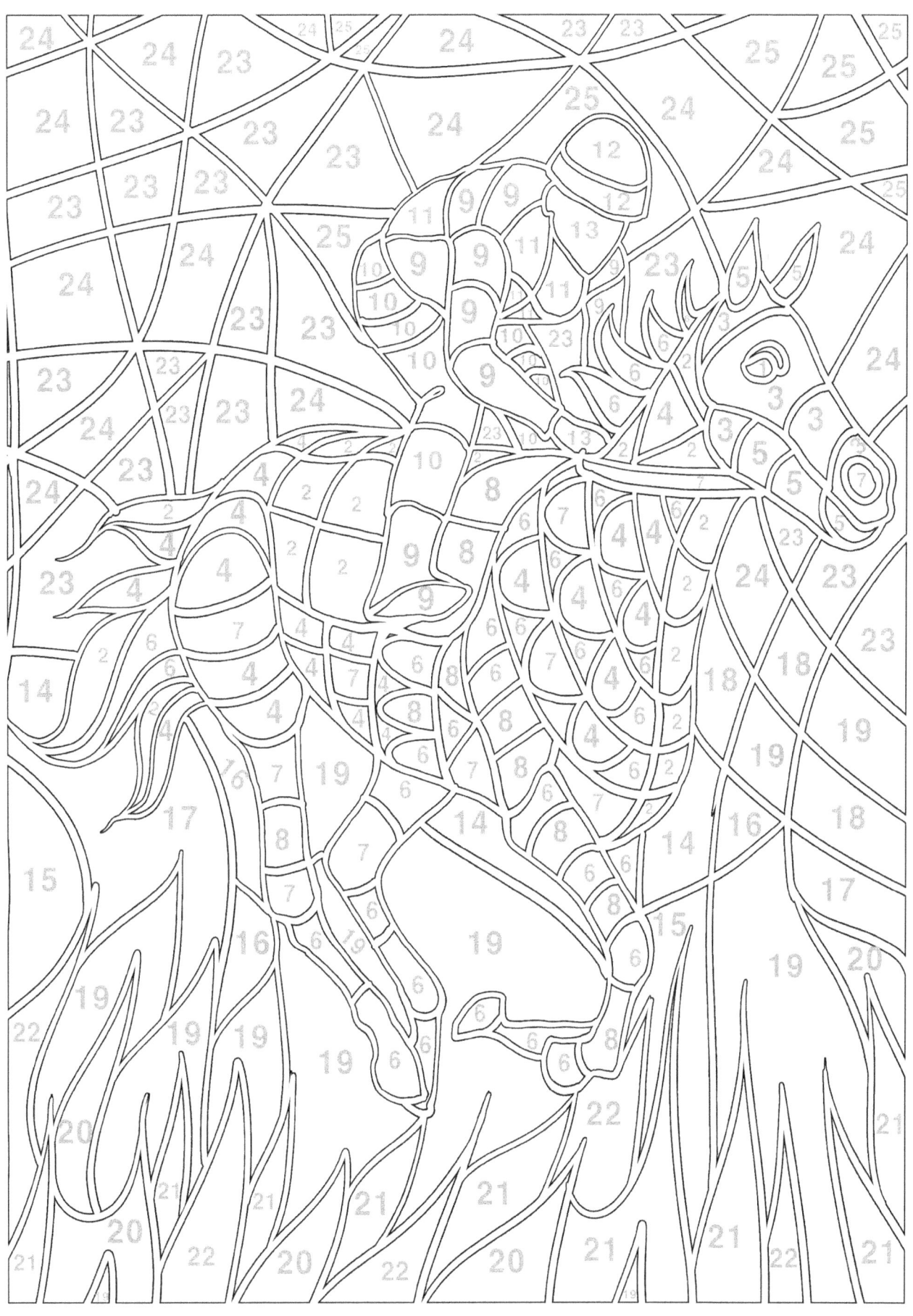

1. Yellow

2. Light Brown

3. Dark brown

4. Light Red

5. Brown

6. Dark Orange

7. Orange

8. Dark Red

9. Light Yellow

10. Yellow

11. White

12. Black

13. Light green

14. green

15. Army Green

16. Light blue

17. Navy Blue

18. Sky Blue

19. Dark blue

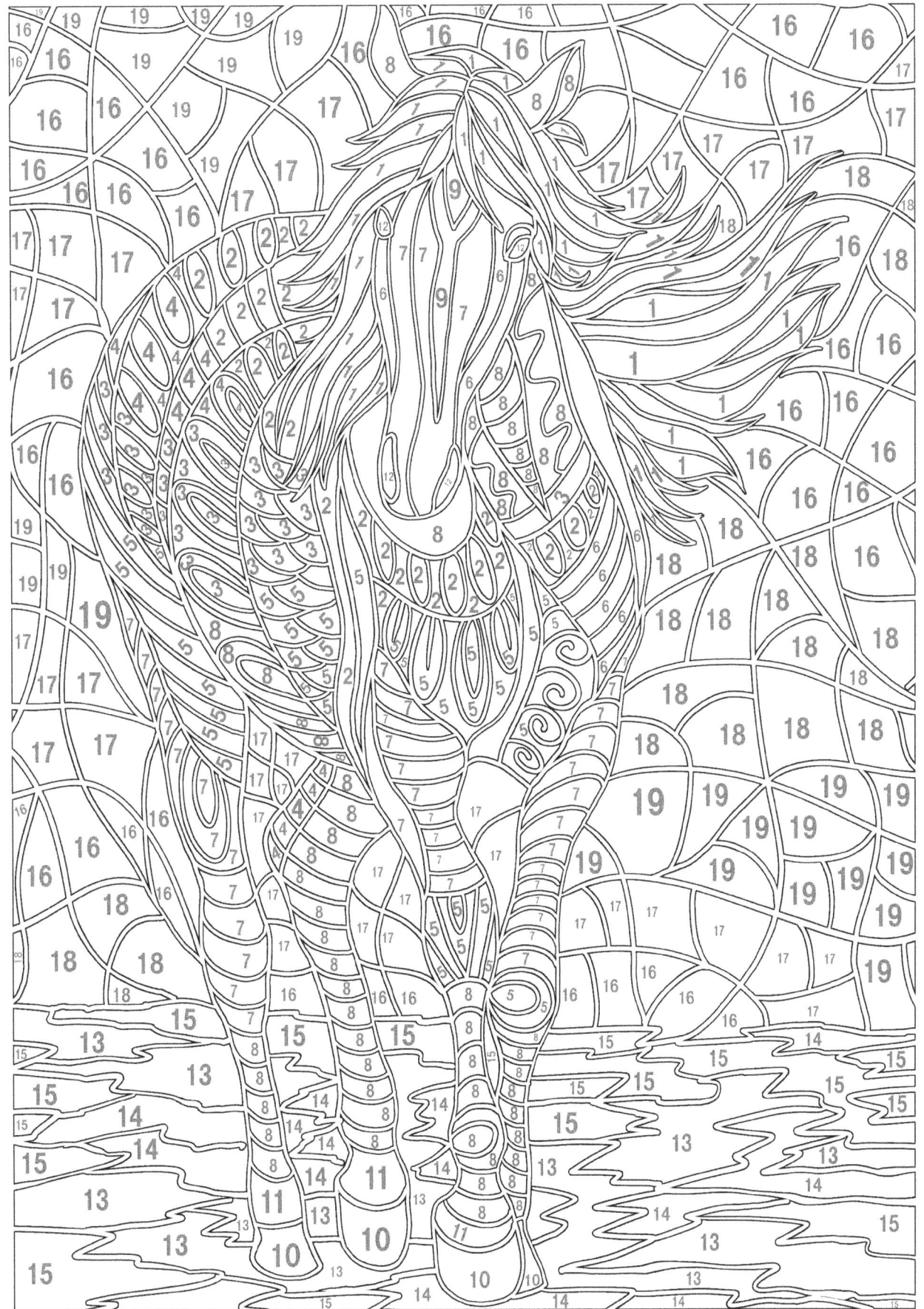

Country Farm Scenes
Nature, Animal, and Easy Designs
Adult Coloring Book
Color By Number For Adults

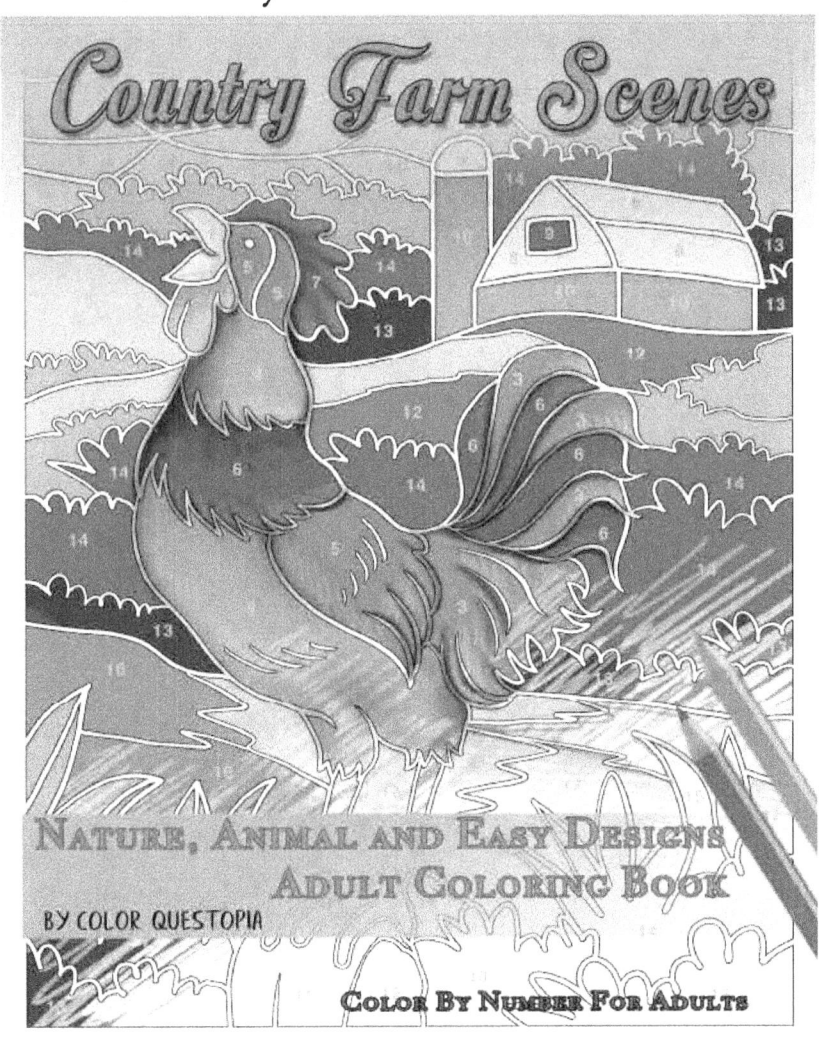

1. Black
2. Dark Brown
3. Pink
4. Brown
5. Light Pink
6. Light Brown
7. Dark Green
8. Medium Green
9. Green
10. Light Green
11. Dark Green
12. Neon Green
13. Army Green
14. Gray
15. Light Gray
16. Blue
17. Light Blue
18. Navy Blue
19. Baby blue

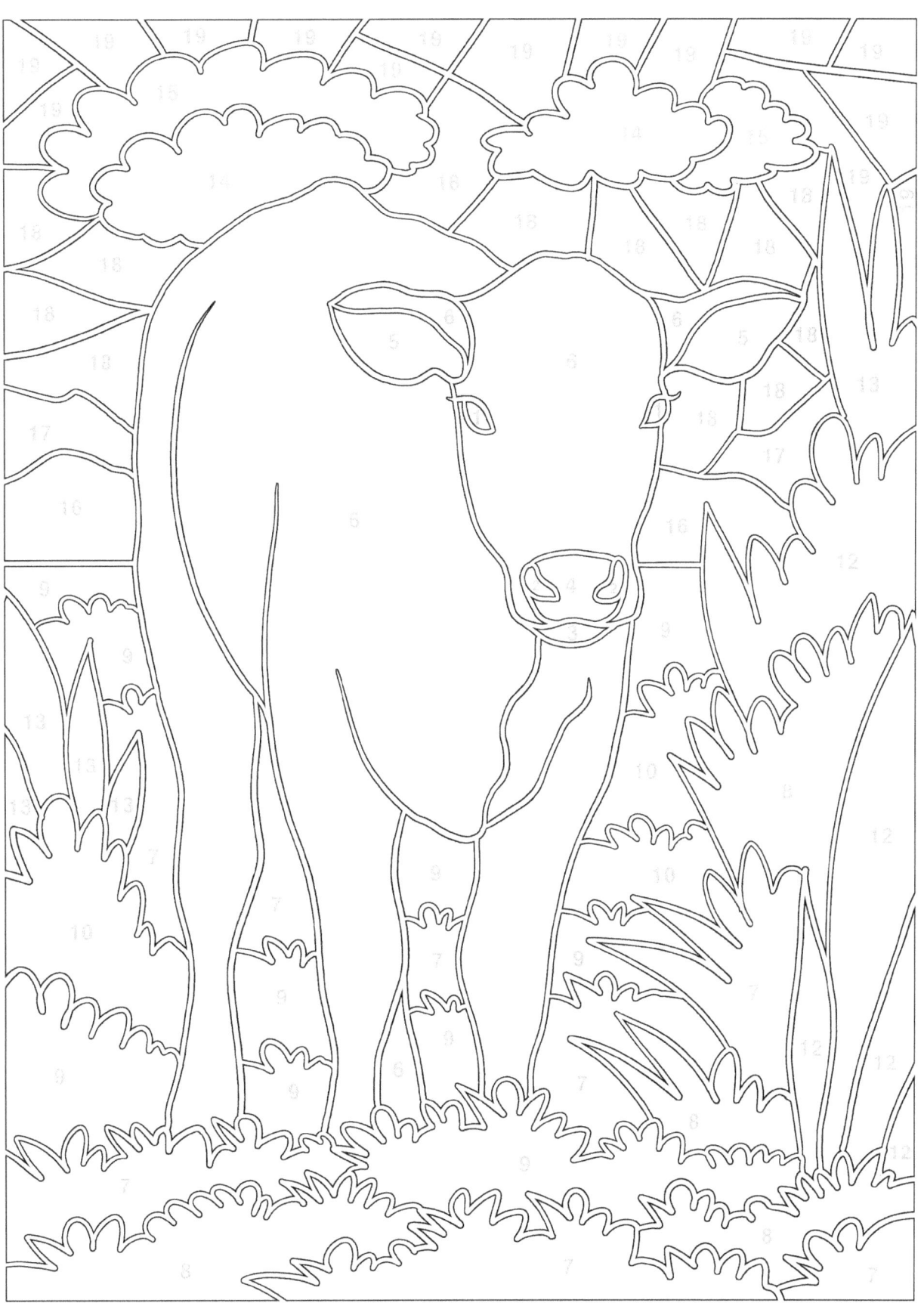

1. Yellow
2. Red
3. Light Yellow
4. Orange
5. Dark Orange
6. Medium blue
7. Navy Blue
8. Light Brown
9. Green
10. Light Green
11. Neon Green
12. Medium Purple
13. Light Purple
14. Medium Gray
15. Gray
16. Light Gray
17. Light Blue

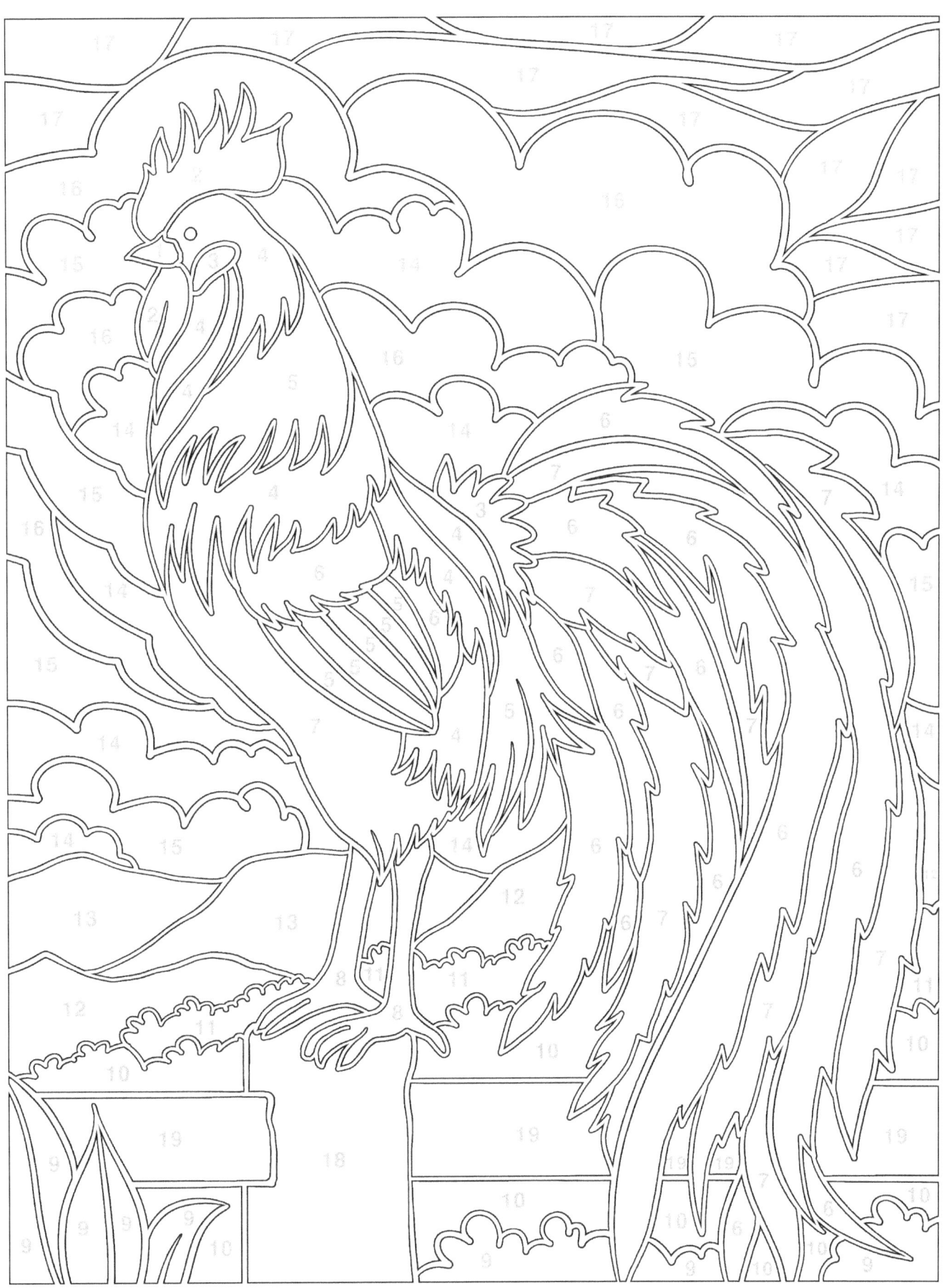

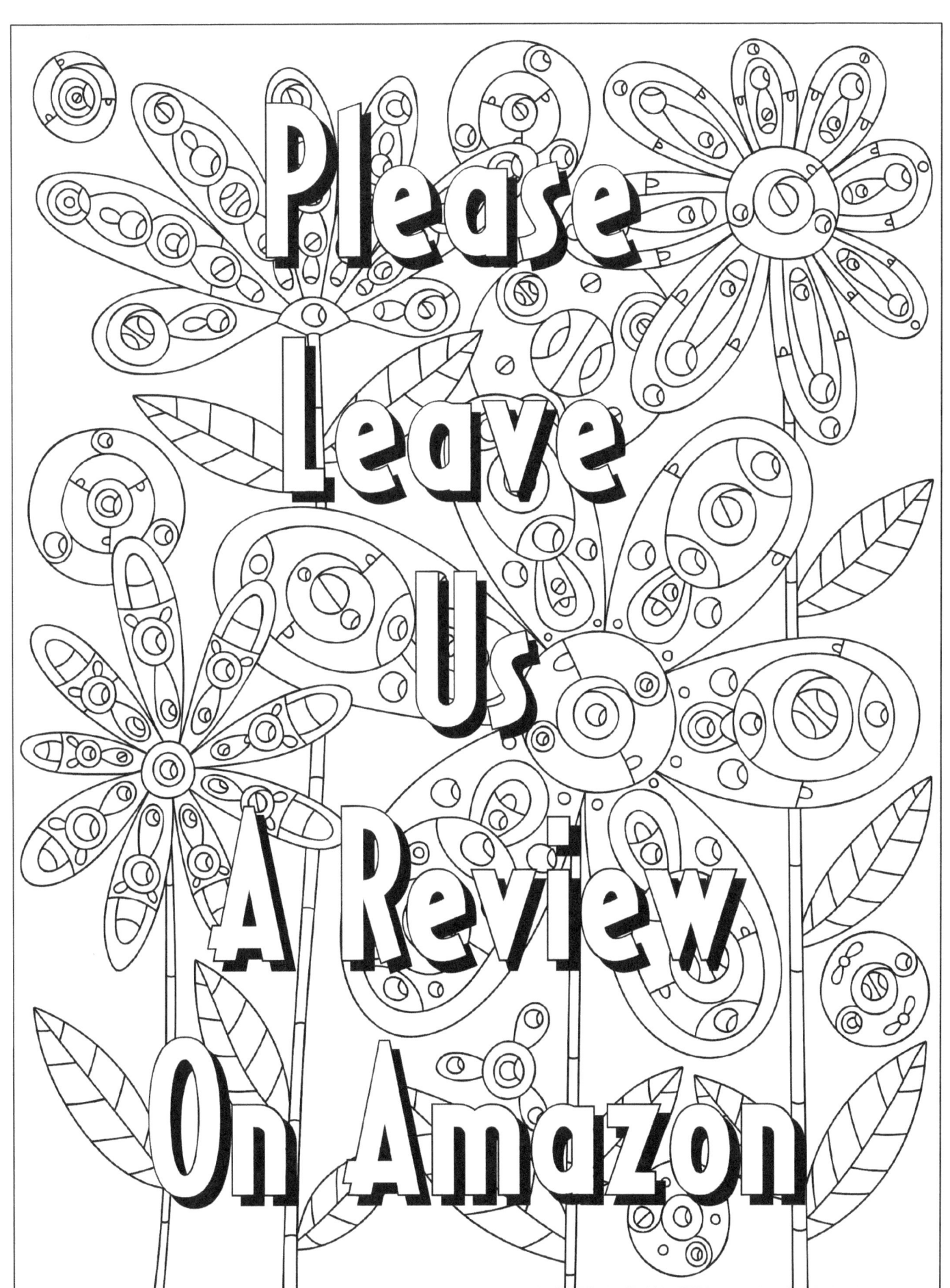